Business Wargaming

Business Wargaming

Securing Corporate Value

DANIEL F. ORIESEK and
JAN OLIVER SCHWARZ

GOWER

Published by
Gower Publishing Limited
Gower House
Croft Road
Aldershot
Hampshire GU11 3HR
England

Ashgate Publishing Company
Suite 420
101 Cherry Street
Burlington, VT 05401-4405
USA

Daniel F. Oriesek and Jan Oliver Schwarz have asserted their moral right under the Copyright, Designs and Patents Act, 1988, to be identified as the authors of this work.

www.gowerpublishing.com

British Library Cataloguing in Publication Data
Oriesek, Daniel F.
 Business wargaming : securing corporate value
 1. Strategic planning 2. Business planning
 I. Title II. Schwarz, Jan Oliver
 658.4'012

ISBN: 978-0-566-08837-7

Library of Congress Cataloging-in-Publication Data
Oriesek, Daniel F.
 Business wargaming : securing corporate value / by Daniel Oriesek and Jan Oliver Schwarz.
  p. cm.
 Includes bibliographical references and index.
 ISBN 978-0-566-08837-7
 1. Management games. 2. Strategic planning--Simulation games. 3. War games. I. Schwarz, Jan Oliver. II. Title.

 HD30.26.O75 2008
 658.4'012--dc22

                                                                      2008010608

Mixed Sources
Product group from well-managed
forests and other controlled sources
www.fsc.org Cert no. SGS-COC-2482
© 1996 Forest Stewardship Council
FSC

Printed and bound in Great Britain by
TJ International Ltd, Padstow, Cornwall.

Contents

List of Figures

List of Abbreviations

2G	second generation
3G	third generation
AIDS	Acquired Immune Deficiency Syndrome
AMA	American Management Association
BC	before Christ
CEO	Chief Executive Officer
CII	Confederation of Indian Industry
DSL	Digital Subscriber Line
e.g.	for example
etc.	et cetera
GBC	Global Business Coalition on HIV/AIDS
GDP	Gross Domestic Product
GSM	Global System for Mobile communications
HIV	Human Immunodeficiency Virus
HMO	Health Maintenance Organization
i.e.	that is
IFPI	International Federation of the Phonographic Industry

IT	Information's Technology
KPIs	Key Performance Indicators
M&A	Mergers and Acquisitions
MBA	Master of Business Administration
Mbit/s	Megabit per second
MIT	Massachusetts Institute of Technology
MMS	Multimedia Messaging Service
MNOs	Mobile Network Operators
NGOs	Non-governmental Organizations
PEST	Political, Economical, Social, Technological
R&D	Research and Development
ret.	retired
SDI	Strategic Defense Initiative
SIM	Subscriber Identity Module Card
SWOT	Strengths, Weaknesses, Opportunities, Threats
TLS	Thought Leadership Summit
UMTS	Universal Mobile Telecommunication System
US	United States
USP	Unique Selling Proposition
USSR	Union of Soviet Socialist Republics
vs.	versus
WLAN	Wireless Local Area Network

Foreword

For a long time wargaming was the province of the military, where it was used to form and test strategies, shake down new concepts for their feasibility, and anticipate a rival's moves. But broadly speaking wargaming was little used in business.

That this is rapidly changing has created the need for a book that describes the nuts and bolts of running a game and the way to design exactly what you want to see in one. *Business Wargaming: Securing Corporate Value* thus makes a timely appearance. More, this book puts wargaming in a larger framework of issues of the highest concern to today's firms. Corporate strategy, change management, and technology integration get an enormous amount of attention. But they are rarely considered from the perspective of this book: how do you game them out?

Let's explore this question a bit more. Behind it lies the fundamental reason for gaming. Unlike any other approach gaming has a singular advantage. This advantage is one likely to appeal to the practicing manager because s/he knows from experience something which is never touched on by other methods. *Business wargaming shows you things you haven't thought about before.* Putting plans to the test in a game, against smart opponents eager to find holes in it and searching for counters to it, gets at what usually goes wrong in strategies: things you haven't thought of. Short of going live – actually launching the new plan or venture – wargaming shows in raw form the many things that are not thought about. It's far better to learn about these in a conference room before the event than it is to learn about them the hard way.

Business wargaming is a form of *accelerated* learning. In today's world, as this book makes clear, it is hard to imagine what could be more valuable. From a wide range of studies about how people learn we know several things. Classroom lectures, slide shows, and committees are not very good at discovering what we don't know. Scenarios may help. And as Oriesek and

Schwarz emphasize here, there is a close relationship between scenarios and wargames. But scenarios used alone suffer from a defect. They are limited by the imagination and foresight of the individual scenario writer. Wargaming overcomes this. By bringing intelligent opponents into the mix a much more realistic dynamic is created.

Ask the following question about your organization: What would be the value if you could accelerate learning by a factor of two, four, or ten? The reason for including the military background to wargaming, in Chapter 1, is because it answers this question. In the minds of the greatest military geniuses, wargaming was useful not only because it exposed opportunities and weakness, but because it did so rapidly. It was possible to learn in a game quickly, in a domain where time was a decisive factor in winning or losing.

Please keep one more consideration in mind as you read this book. Your organization already plays games. In fact, it plays very important games. These are the games in people's heads as they react to competitive pressures and management changes. In many respects these are the most important games played of all. The trouble is that these games are decentralized, distributed throughout the organization. Usually they are only coordinated during coffee breaks and in brief snippets of conversation as your employees leave the conference room. Wargaming systematizes this knowledge, it gets it out in the table for everyone to see and work with.

Pulling all of these issues together, and combining it with a manual for actually running your own games, is a major achievement. As the business world becomes ever more turbulent, the timing for *Business Wargaming: Securing Corporate Value* couldn't be better.

Paul Bracken
Professor, Yale School of Management

Introduction

The only constant is change, continuing change, inevitable change, that is the dominant factor in society today. No sensible decision can be made any longer without taking into account not only the world as it is, but the world as it will be.

This quote by science fiction author Isaac Asimov (Hartung 2004) precisely captures the challenge decision makers are increasingly facing, namely having to take decisions in ever more complex and instable environments, while the magnitude of the consequences triggered by their decisions are, for the most part, ever increasing. Some of the decisions made today are literally "bet your company" types of decisions; the decision to opt for a particular technology, which may generate significant revenue or may be obsolete before you have even completed its implementation.

We firmly believe that in situations too complex for conventional (i.e. mostly linear) forms of analysis, business wargaming (a methodology developed originally in a military context), offers today's top decision makers a way, if not to eliminate, at least to reduce the uncertainty they face when making decisions. A business wargame is a role-playing simulation of a dynamic business situation (Kurtz 2003). It involves several teams, each assigned to play a different stakeholder (competitor, customer, governing bodies) in a particular business situation. Typically a business wargame evolves over several moves. Each move represents a defined period of time. A business wargame should always be prefaced by extensive research and include a review of trends and hypotheses' for the particular industry in which the wargame is taking place.

The term "wargame" is the translation of the German *Kriegsspiel*. Since many people in the military feel uncomfortable with using the term *game* (because of the gravity of war), wargames have been called many things, including map maneuvers, field maneuvers, exercises, or increasingly, modeling and simulations. As in the business environment some discomfort exists with the terms "war" and "game" alike, wargames therefore have also been described as dynamic strategic simulations or simply strategy simulations. For simplicity and authenticity, we will stick to the term "wargame" in this book.

While setting up and conducting a business wargame does not come cheap, the cost of a game should ultimately be only a fraction of the cost you may otherwise incur through poor decision making or the additional revenue potential of previously unrecognized opportunities. We therefore chose the subtitle for our book to be "Securing Corporate Value", because it captures exactly what business wargaming can do for the company if done right. On the one hand, you can look at the process opportunistically and say, business wargaming will confirm or uncover areas for future growth which will allow you to secure a piece of that opportunity otherwise ignored; or you can look at it more defensively by viewing business wargaming as a tool to avoid costly mistakes, such as acquisitions which for whatever reason just won't work, or technology expenditures that fail to generate a marketable product or service in the end.

In this book we have tried to give you a very practical overview of business wargaming and how it can be applied. Part I opens by summarizing the history and the background to business wargaming. In Chapter 1, we spend time discussing the history of military wargaming, starting with the earliest applications and highlighting the development of military wargaming during the Prussian era and subsequently, after World War II, in the United States (US) military. Since the rise of business wargaming can be also credited to the US military and US hobby wargaming tradition, the emphasis will be on these fields. Chapter 2 will explain the mechanics of wargaming, referring here to the application of business wargaming for strategy testing. In Chapter 3 we emphasize the role of business wargaming for strategy formulation. The reason for highlighting the role of business wargaming in strategy at this early stage is because we believe that including business wargaming in a strategic planning process represents its most valuable application. We also feel that this discussion enables us to highlight the development of business wargaming as a tool for management in a turbulent and uncertain environment.

The aim of Part II is to present a variety of specific applications of business wargaming. Whilst not seeking to cover the entire field of possible applications, this overview provides the reader with a good grounding in the most common applications of the technique. We have added case studies to each application to help explain in more detail how business wargaming can be applied in the particular context. The examples represent wargames that have been designed and conducted by the authors themselves or by third party organizations, primarily consulting firms such as Booz Allen Hamilton, who have been active in the field of commercial wargaming for over 20 years. The information provided from such third party games has either been written up and published or communicated during public presentations. Some of the examples are very detailed, while others remain more general as the specific findings remain proprietary to the organizations that commissioned the games and are not for public disclosure.

We open Chapter 4 with the process of testing strategies through business wargames, including case examples from the private sector as well as a brief note on an application in the military field. In Chapter 5 we discuss how business wargaming can be applied for crisis response preparation; highlighting two very interesting public-sector case studies and one case from the private sector. In Chapter 6 we turn to an application of business wargaming which addresses the notion and the need for corporations and organizations in general to develop foresight in an increasingly dynamic and complex environment. The case study in this chapter describes how a business wargame was applied to give representatives of the asset management industry an opportunity to make sense of the future of their industry. We also briefly outline in this chapter how business wargaming was used during the Cold War to develop foresight with respect to shifts in global power structures.

Chapter 7 covers the topic of applying business wargaming in the context of change management. Whilst we are only able to provide a short case study here, it does underline how business wargames, regardless of the specific application, can help to understand why change is needed and how an organization can prepare through simulation for a major change effort.

In Chapter 8 we turn to training and recruitment as an application. In particular, we will highlight how business wargaming can be used as a recruiting tool, with reference to the Booz Allen CEO Challenge, and how business wargaming can be applied in a university context to teach strategic management to masters-level students.

The two subsequent chapters are aimed at providing further applications for business wargaming as well as an alternative approach to designing and executing a business wargame. In Chapter 9 we describe two areas we believe could be promising for applying business wargaming methodology: strategic early warning systems and corporate reputation. Finally, in Chapter 10 Pero Mićić, chairman of the German-based FutureManagementGroup, describes an approach to designing and executing a business wargame, which offers a different perspective on the design and execution from the approach we have described thus far.

Chapter 11 in Part III discusses a number of issues around the design and execution of a business wargame, drawing on our experience. This is not intended to be a "How to" chapter, but should rather provide food for thought, so that you are in a position to think creatively how business wargaming could help your organization as a starting point to commissioning an actual game.

Finally, we would like to thank the following people for their contributions, insights and inspiration: George E. Thibault, Mark Frost and all the other wargamers at Booz Allen Hamilton; Prof. Paul Bracken from the Yale School of Management; Pero Mićić from the FutureManagementGroup; Brigadier Marcel Fantoni and Colonel Christoph Pfister of the Swiss Armed Forces General Staff School; and Jonathan Norman from Gower Publishing who did a brilliant job in supporting us on our journey towards writing this book. And we would also like to thank our significant others, Romana Oriesek and Victoria von Groddeck, for their support and understanding providing us with the necessary time and energy to complete this work.

Daniel F. Oriesek and Jan Oliver Schwarz
February 2008

PART I

Background to Business Wargaming

The History of Wargaming

The development and employment of wargaming reaches far back in time and is probably as old as war itself (Perla 1990). Wargaming most likely grew out of a military necessity, namely to better prepare military leaders and their officers for unforeseen developments on the battlefield. The ability to better understand what likely hostile reactions one's own planned course of action would evoke and how to best counter these reactions constitutes a source of competitive advantage, because such knowledge helps the commander to avoid fatal decisions that would result in unnecessary losses of soldiers, equipment and territory. This in turn allows for a more "economic" way of warfare, which would significantly raise the sustainability of any military campaign, in essence ensuring that an army does not only "win the battle" but ultimately "wins the war." Another likely driver for the proliferation of wargaming was the opportunity to test new doctrines and tactics without actually engaging in combat. This proved especially valuable in refining the art of warfare during peacetime and training thousands of new officers in a uniform way of thinking. Of course there are more advantages to wargaming, but the above are the most significant ones up to this date.

The existing literature on wargaming (e.g. Brewer and Shubik 1979; Perla 1990; Treat *et al*. 1996; Dunnigan 2000; Caffrey Jr 2000; Oriesek and Friedrich 2003) focuses on three fields: first, the application of wargaming in the US military, in particular at the Naval War College; second the development of wargaming in Prussian Germany; and third, the use of wargaming by civilians as a hobby. The application of wargaming in a business context, also called business wargaming is, in comparison to the overall evolution of the methodology, a recent development, which is also reflected in the fact that currently very little literature is available on the subject. We will start with the earliest accounts of wargaming and highlight its development over time up to the current day.

Wei-Hai and Go in Ancient China

Perla (1990) credits the Chinese general and military philosopher Sun Tzu for developing the first wargame about five thousand years ago, called "Wei-Hai", meaning "encirclement." Wei-Hai used an abstract playing surface on which each of the contestants maneuvered their armies of colored stones. Reflecting on Sun Tzu's philosophy of resorting to the chances of battle only as a last resort, victory went not to the player who could bludgeon his opponent head-on, but to the first player who could outflank his enemy (Perla 1990). While no pictures or artifacts are available of this particular game it appears that it was quite similar to the game of "Go" which we still know today and which was developed around 2200 BC. Go is an abstract strategy game which is played on a wooden board consisting of a 19 × 19 matrix using black and white stones. It spread throughout the Orient and underwent further extensive developments in both Japan, where it is known as "I-Go" or simply "Go" (the name now universally applied), and Korea where it is known as "Baduk." The objective of Go is to obtain as much territory as possible on the game board.

From Chaturanga in India to Chess

Around 500 BC a game by the name of "Chaturanga" appeared in India. Like Go, the game consisted of a board, on which colored stones had to be moved around according to specific rules, but the stones were more differentiated than those used in Go, representing different foot soldiers, chariots, elephants, and cavalry. Between two and four players moved four peasants, one king, one elephant, a horse and a chariot over the game board with the objective to capture the hostile figures, not to gain as much space on the board as possible. With the help of a dice-like device, the outcome of the moves and encounters of different figures (e.g. chariot beats foot soldier or vice-versa) were determined. The interesting aspect of Chaturanga is that now not only stones or figures with different value were introduced, but that with the use of a dice, an element of randomness or uncertainty was introduced as well. This game made its way to Persia and most writers agree that Chaturanga is the forerunner of what we today know as "chess."

Chess and Further Developments

The modern game of chess was mentioned for the first time in the thirteenth century in southern Europe. It is believed that Arabs, known as Moors, learned chess from the Persians when they invaded Persia in the eighth century and later brought the game to Europe when they invaded Spain. From Spain chess quickly spread across Europe. The Europeans gave chess pieces the names we know today, in part because they had a hard time in pronouncing and spelling the Persian names, but also to reflect the world and the hierarchy in which they lived.

The pawns on the chessboard represent serfs, or laborers. There are more of them than any other piece on the board, and often they are sacrificed to save the more valuable pieces. In medieval times, serfs were considered no more than the property of landowners—chattels. Life was brutally hard for serfs during this era of history. They worked hard and died young. They were often left unprotected while wars raged around them. They could be traded, used as a diversion, or even sacrificed to allow the landowners to escape harm. The castle signifies the home, or the refuge, just as it was a home in medieval times. The knight represents the professional soldier of medieval times whose job it was to protect persons of rank; knights are more important than pawns, but less important than bishops, kings, or queens. Their purpose in the game is to protect the more important pieces, and they can be sacrificed to save those pieces. There are two bishops in the game, who represent the Church. The Church was a rich and powerful force in medieval times, and religion played a large part in every person's life. The queen is the only piece on the board that represents a woman, and she is the most powerful piece of the game. There is only one queen for each side. The king is the most important, but not the most powerful piece in chess. He is as well defended on the chessboard as in medieval life. In medieval times, the surrender of the king would mean the loss of the kingdom to invading armies and that could mean change for the worse. It was to everyone's advantage, from the lowest serf to the highest-ranking official, to keep the king safe from harm. Although chess is characterized by a high degree of abstraction, it contains the typical elements of contemporary warfare. However, with the introduction of firearms in the seventeenth century, chess lost its value for military simulations, as was quickly recognized by the leading military strategists, and so new forms of wargaming had to be developed.

In 1664 Christopher Weikhmann developed an advanced chess game, which reflected more military details in Ulm, Germany. His game was called "Königsspiel" or "King's Game" and, compared with ordinary chess, this game was played on a larger board and comprised more figures. The King's Game, as well as other more military-oriented versions of chess, also known as "Military Chess" or "War Chess", represented more complex versions of the traditional chess game. Weikhmann intended his game not only for entertainment purposes, but foremost as a tool for those who were interested and wanted to study military as well as political structures and workings.

However, it remains doubtful that the complex and abstract King's Game was ever employed by the military for training purposes. Although the King's Game and other games belonging to the group of war chess were of little practical use to the military and constituted rudimentary simulations at best, the elements used to play them led to the introduction of three principles which up to this day are considered of vital importance to any wargaming simulation. Although it is not possible to trace back when the different elements were exactly introduced for the first time, all three of them could be found in a new game, developed by the German Dr. C.L. Helwig, intended to introduce more realism into the game.

These three principles were: first, the change that now a game figure represented a larger contingent of soldiers and no longer individuals; second, replacing the two-colored game board with a multicolored game board, representing different terrains; and third, a referee was installed to run the game and watch over its proper execution. As a teacher and educator at the court of the Count of Braunschweig, Helwig used his game to educate his students in military thinking and decision making. Although his game represented a major innovation, it was still strongly influenced by chess, but was successful in as far as it was copied beyond the borders of Germany and played by noblemen in France, Italy and Austria alike.

Games for Military Use

Around approximately the same time as Dr. C.L. Helwig developed his game, the Scotsman John Clerk invented a method to simulate ship battles, which was effectively the first naval wargame. Clerk's aim was to analyze the moves and tactics of battle ships in more detail and thus he not only studied their tactics, but also performed mathematical calculations in order to determine the firepower of the ship guns and the possible damage they could cause. John Clerk's conclusions were published in 1790, under the title: *An Essay on Naval Tactics, Systematic and Historic*. One simple advantage of his game setup was that no model of the terrain was needed. In fact a simple table would suffice to simulate the surface of the ocean. Copies of Clerk's work were distributed to influential naval decision makers, including Admiral Sir George Rodney. Later Rodney credited Clerk's tactics as one of the causes for British success against the French fleet in the West Indies. It is reported that Lord Nelson employed variations of Clerk's tactics in 1797 off Cape St. Vincent and also in his victory at Trafalgar in 1805.

At the end of the eighteenth century, the Schleswig-born scholar and military author Georg Venturini set out to develop a new wargame. In 1796 he published the book *Regeln für ein Neues Kriegsspiel für den Gebrauch an Militärlehranstalten* or *Rules for a new Wargame for Use at Military Educational Institutions*. Venturini, like Helwig, also used a game board, consisting of quadrants, but in comparison to Helwig and others his game board was significantly larger, consisting of 3600 fields, each representing one square mile and in total representing a chosen terrain, namely the border between Belgium and France.

In his game the players could not only simulate various troops, but also the use of equipment, strongholds, bridges and depots. Unlike in a chess game, where figures could easily move from one field to another, Venturini's game applied a high degree of realism with respect to how fast and easy elements could be moved from one field to another contingent on the underlying territory. The game was used in particular for military education at various military academies. Due to its size and complexity, it could not be played outside of military settings.

The nineteenth century was characterized by a growth in troop sizes, which made real-life exercises and relocations more difficult as well as by a number of industrial developments, which made fighting more complex. On the one hand, the weapons of the infantry and the guns of the artillery had ever longer firing ranges, precision and firing cadences and, on the other hand, the introduction of the machine gun in the late nineteenth century offered a totally new form of fire power, which significantly changed the game for attackers and defenders alike. Furthermore, the construction of a dense railway infrastructure now offered ways to more quickly move and concentrate entire armies.

At the same time contemporary societies, first and foremost in Prussian Germany, became increasingly "militarized" and the study of military affairs was perceived to be "chic" especially among the commoners of the time. The rise in popularity of wargaming in the nineteenth century can be credited especially to the Baron von Reisswitz, not a soldier but a civilian war counselor. He replaced the centrepiece of many games thus far, the two-dimensional game board, with a sandbox, in which three-dimensional models of the terrain could be replicated. Von Reisswitz further introduced wooden game pieces, which represented the actual size of military formations to scale.

In doing so, the simulations gained additional realism. Furthermore, von Reisswitz introduced the use of scenarios, placing the players in a particular situation at the outset of the game. Through a lucky coincidence, von Reisswitz introduced the two sons of the Prussian King Friedrich Wilhelm II, Friedrich and Wilhelm (who later became Kaiser Wilhelm I), to his wargame and in 1811 and 1812 respectively von Reisswitz even had the opportunity to demonstrate his wargame to King Friedrich Wilhelm II personally, who was impressed. However, von Reisswitz's game never became widely popular because it was simply too bulky and difficult to move to different locations.

The original "von Reisswitz" wargame was significantly enhanced when his son, Georg Heinrich Rudolf Johann von Reisswitz, replaced the bulky sandbox with a topographical map modelled to a 1:1800 scale. Georg, who had served as a first lieutenant in the Prussian artillery, attempted to codify actual military experience and introduced the details of real-life military operations into the game, a factor missing in his father's version. The rulebook for the game now included all imaginable military operations, starting at the company level all the way up to the division and corps level. This rulebook was published in 1824 under the title *Anleitung zur Darstellung militärischer Manöver mit dem Apparat des Kriegsspiels*, or *Instructions for the Representation of Military Maneuvers by Use of Wargaming*. It is at this point that the term *wargaming* came into existence and there was a decisive breakthrough in its application when von Reisswitz was given the opportunity to present his game to the Chief of the General Staff of the Prussian Army, von Müffling. Historians record that on observing the demonstration von Müffling shouted: "This is not a game! This is a preparation for war! I need to recommend this to be rolled out to the whole army" (Perla 1990, 26). He then published a very favorable article in the *Berlin Military Week*, a highly regarded publication.

The "Kriegsspiel" or wargame was played on a topographical map with little metal figures that could be moved, representing military formations. The rules of the game included details on exactly how these figures could be moved, details on how battles would be carried out and in addition a referee was appointed to watch over these rules and resolve any issues. Over the course of the following years the "Kriegsspiel" gained popularity, yet it was criticized for allowing junior officers a simulated taste of commanding forces well beyond their rank, which, in turn would cause them to lose a sense of reality and be less ambitious in performing their assigned tasks. Over time, with the introduction of new and more complex weapon systems, the rules for the game grew so complex that it could only be executed with the help of wargaming experts. Although, on the one hand, great progress was made in trying to simulate ever more details of the actual realities of war, on the other hand the system of increasing detail and pseudo-exactitude detracted from the very realism that the game had hoped to improve (Perla 1990).

Nevertheless, wargaming became popular beyond Prussia in countries such as the US, Great Britain, Italy, France, Russia, and Japan. This popularity was to a large extent driven by the fact that the Chief of the Prussian General Staff under the high command of General Gebhard Blücher, Gerhard von Scharnhorst, made extensive use of wargaming to simulate the moves of his own troops and the likely reactions of Napoleon as a way of preparing his very modest resources for battle. Ironically von Scharnhorst died before Napoleon and his troops were finally defeated, but the success of the Prussians is in no small part attributed to his preparations using wargaming.

However, the complexity in the Prussian "Kriegsspiel" led in 1876 to Prussian Colonel Jules von Verdy du Vernois pointing out that the reason for the lack of popularity of wargaming was due to the numerous difficulties that beginners encountered when handling tables, calculating losses and so forth. In contrast to von Reisswitz's "Kriegsspiel" he proposed the "Free Kriegsspiel", characterized by replacing many of the rigid rules by a regulator who would explain his actions and assessments after the game. Although enthusiastically accepted and applied by those who found the rigid games too complex and boring, "Free Kriegsspiel" had its own problems. The connection between the proponents of rigid and free "Kriegsspiel" brought into sharper focus the tension between realism and playability. More important, it revealed the fact that the lack of realism could result in a lack of playability, just as lack of playability could lead to a shortage of realism. The late nineteenth and early twentieth centuries thus began to see increased efforts to achieve some sort of balance between the false realism of "Rigid Kriegsspiel" and the false playability of "Free Kriegsspiel" (Perla 1990).

Up to this point in history, the wargaming used in the military was primarily focused on training and educating its participants, be it in specific military tactics, educating them about a doctrine for using new weapon systems or simply fostering an understanding for military matters. With the ongoing "industrialization" of warfare came the recognition in the late nineteenth and early twentieth century that successful warfare no longer was a simple matter of superior tactics, but increasingly of superior logistics. What really mattered now was who could mobilize and deploy his troops faster than the enemy and thus have them on time, in the right location with the right equipment. The emphasis on wargaming to test mobilization scenarios increased, for one because it was indeed a key success factor to successful engagement of the enemy, but also because the size of armies was ever growing and thus full-scale mobilization exercises just weren't a viable way to practice.

Mobilization wargaming could be considered the first shift away from pure training and education games towards games with the purpose of analyzing and studying specific problems of military operations (Perla 1990). This development was mainly driven by the German Army, which recognized early on that wargaming was in fact far more broadly applicable than just for educating and training tactics. This recognition also led the Germans to elevate the simulation approach to the operative, even strategic level by pioneering a new form of gaming, known as political–military wargames. In those games political factors were built into the game, which could very well influence the outcome of a campaign.

In 1879 when Germany was at the height of its application of wargaming, W.R. Livermore introduced a German-style of wargaming to the United States with his publication *The American Kriegsspiel*. Livermore's system was a derivative of the "Rigid Kriegsspiel" and was clearly indebted to the German school. In the opinion of some American soldiers it was not appropriate to the unique conditions of the United States. One of the most outspoken critics was Lieutenant Charles A.L. Totten, who in 1880 published his own book on wargaming techniques, *Strategos: A Series of American Games of War Based upon Military Principles*. There is little evidence that wargaming was used in the US at the time apart from for training and education purposes. Perla (1990) concludes that neither the British nor the Americans ever quite accepted the full range of wargaming potential value prior to the end of World War II. The only notable exception in the US is the Naval War College in Rhode Island.

Established in 1884 with the aim of transforming the Navy into a true profession and turning the Navy's officers into well-educated, well-rounded masters of the tools and techniques of the unique naval art, the Naval War College encountered difficulties executing training maneuvers, because of a lack of funds and therefore had to resort to wargaming in order to train its naval officers. In 1887 McCarthy Little, who had been influenced by Livermore's *The American Kriegsspiel*, expanded his single lectures of the previous year into a series of six presentations and conducted the first actual wargame at the Naval War College. Wargaming became part of the regular curriculum at the college and experienced a rise in popularity and prominence, due to wide media coverage.

Following World War I the wargaming activities at the Naval War College were faced with the challenge of the increasing complexity of naval warfare due to the rising prominence of submarines and aircraft in battles at sea. Up to this point in time, naval wargames were based on the assumption that all ships had similar characteristics for the purpose of damage assessment in the game. This assumption had to be modified to reflect the recent developments in naval warfare and the repertoire of resources had to be enriched by adding submarines and aircraft. Yet the main purpose of the wargames which followed these modifications at the college was still education; providing the players with decision-making experiences.

After World War II, the number of wargames conducted at the Naval War College was reduced, but wargaming remained an important element of the curriculum. Over the years, the strict rules of the initial wargames were relaxed or replaced by less rigid ones. Increasingly, the games became tailored to the objectives, the level, and the scope of each separate scenario. Emerging computer technology in the 1950s revolutionized wargaming at the college. In 1958 the Navy Electronic Warfare Simulator was introduced, becoming the post-World War II successor to the game board and chart maneuvers introduced by McCarty Little in the 1880s. The system was built around a large-screen display that dominated the bottom floor of the facility and served as the principal tool by which the control team kept track of the action. The second floor contained shops and air-conditioned equipment, but also had a balcony overlooking the "game floor" and a small conference room. The third floor was the player area, composed of the various command centers.

In the following years interest in the wargaming of the Naval War College grew consistently, particularly with the introduction of the Navy Electronic Warfare Simulator, which was further improved by advances in computer technology. In addition to purely educational purposes, wargaming was now increasingly used for other reasons too. Wargames were used to familiarize participating staff members with an operation prior to an at-sea exercise or deployment on a mission. It was also found most useful as a means by which to experiment with new tactics, combat formations, testing command-and-control structures, and exploring possible effects of enemy counteractions to planned courses of action. Alongside the broadening applications, wargaming was increasingly integrated with other forms of research at the Naval War College. Driven by new technological developments such as increased processor speed, parallel processing, visual interfaces, and networking capabilities, the wargames have become ever more refined up to the present day.

Non-military Wargaming and Recent Developments

Although most of the history of wargaming is centered on military applications, it is worthwhile spending a few lines on the history of wargaming outside the military context. Even in Prussian times, wargames caught the attention of non-military personnel and elsewhere in Europe interest groups emerged, such as the first wargaming club in England, founded by Spenser Wilkinson at the end of the nineteenth century. It is further reported that a member of Parliament stated "wargaming" as one of his hobbies in 1900 (Caffrey Jr 2000). However, hobby wargaming did not take off until H.G. Wells published *Floor Games* in 1912 and soon after *Little Wars* in 1913. The latter, described a system using toy soldiers made of lead and a spring-loaded cannon that fired a wooden projectile capable of knocking the men over. The battlefield consisted of a model house, miniature trees, and various other elements. Due to the popularity of his amateur games, Wells is widely perceived as the father of modern miniature wargaming.

With the exception of the Naval War College, armed forces around the world seemed to lose interest in wargaming. In the post-World War II era military research was dominated by civilians, focusing on operations research and systems analysis and so with a few exceptions the traditional discipline of wargaming lost more and more ground and supporters. Wargaming in the military context experienced yet another decline in interest during the Vietnam war, largely due to wargames, which were notoriously flawed and misleading, further shaking the trust in the usefulness of the methodology (Perla 1990). While military applications of wargaming were on the decline, academic strategists and political scientists started to apply wargaming to what was more obviously a less-than-quantifiable subject-political issues and behavior (Perla 1990), leading to the political-military games in the USA, which Germany and Japan had already pioneered during the 1930s.

In parallel to an increasing shift away from pure military wargaming towards political-military games, several hobby wargames began to appear in the US, most prominent of which was "Tactics" developed in 1953 by Charles S. Roberts from Baltimore. Tactics uses a map, on which two hypothetical states are battling for supremacy. The troops are represented by printed card pallets and each troop has a value assigned to it, representing fighting power and action radius. The results of the individual battles, i.e. when troops of one state collided with the troops of another state, could be calculated by using the Combat Result Table and by tossing dice, for random events. Triggered by the success of Tactics, Roberts founded The Avalon Hill Company and produced a total of 18 games up until 1963. Six years later, another dominant company in the gaming space was founded in New York, Simulations Publications Inc. The company produced a wide array of games and published as many as 30 new games per year. A major contribution by Simulations Publications Inc. to hobby games was to add more "realism" to the games by considering factors, such as the firepower of weapons, morale, and military training levels. The recreational market for simulations grew to over 2.2 million games sold in 1980. After its peak in 1980 the number of manual wargames sold consistently declined. Dunnigan (2000) states that with the proliferation of manual games in the 1980s, computer wargames began to take over, selling five to ten times as many copies. Overall, it has become increasingly difficult to differentiate between simulations, models, and games (Bracken and Shubik 2001), making it increasingly difficult to assess the number of wargames sold.

The success of these hobby wargames did not go unnoticed by the US military, which in 1976 contracted Simulations Publication Inc. to produce a game for the US Army Infantry School in Fort Benning by the name of "Firefight." This was later released also to the public. Over the course of the 1990s, hobby wargaming struggled with the declining demand for printed wargames, recovering by switching to software based versions, adding high levels of realism and experience to various forms of simulations from theatre level campaigns to straight forward infantry tactics simulators.

While recreational wargaming was experiencing a boom, military wargaming advanced far more slowly in the 1970s. Perla (1990) states that ever since the introduction in the late nineteenth century the US had become the leading nation in deploying defence analysis and wargaming. Nevertheless, several other nations have and still are using wargaming, especially Japan, the former Soviet Union, and Germany. In particular, the wargaming tradition of the former Soviet Union has influenced wargames conducted by the communist north Vietnamese regime during the Vietnam War and by the Iraqis during the Iraq–Iran war.

Following the example and contributions of the Naval War College, other military branches in the US began to use wargaming. The US Air Force and the Army started applying wargaming techniques after World War II and the Marine Corps established a series of wargames dealing with landing a force ashore in 1958. Wargaming after World War II in the military has been largely influenced by operations research and systems analysis, neglecting the study of history, which had formed the basis of earlier wargames. Dunnigan (2000) points out that the military is now playing wargames, which cater to their specific requirements. During the 1980s the Army and the Air Force established training centers for conducting wargames.

Since the 1960s, the US military has made an increased effort to bring together the various branches of the Armed Forces in joint wargames. In 1961 a formal wargaming operation was established at the Joint Chiefs of Staff level. Following the fiasco at the Bay of Pigs, President John F. Kennedy complained that his military advisers did not understand the political implications of their recommendations. This encouraged the use of political-military wargames at the Pentagon and at professional military education schools (Caffrey Jr 2000). Currently the US military still uses wargaming as a means of validating its military strategies and force structure in an often uncertain future (Haffa and Patton 1999). For example, the National Strategic Gaming Center, located within the Institute for National Strategic Studies at the National Defense University in Washington D.C., designs and conducts wargames for diverse audiences (McCown 2005). In 1999, NATO held a well-attended conference on modeling, simulation, and wargaming, demonstrating that wargaming had become truly international and is used in many joint and even combined settings (Caffrey Jr 2000).

While computer wargames have been growing in popularity, they are not necessarily suitable for all wargames. Particularly at a more strategic level, the focus is less on the quantitative accuracy of model-based calculation, but rather on the larger implication a course of action may have. However, wargaming practitioners report that the level of acceptance of the results of a computer wargame is often higher, in contrast to human adjudicators (McKenna 2003).

The Evolution of Business Wargaming

Following the evolution of wargaming in the military and political context, it seems obvious that after a certain period the business world would discover this tool; particularly as many of the elements of classical military wargames seem transferable. Instead of enemy armies, a company faces competitors; instead of territory, companies battle over market share and profits; instead of artillery and other weapon systems, companies use people, finance, facilities, raw materials, know-how, marketing tools, production processes, and innovation, just to name a few of the resources; and in the place of a referee judging individual military actions, a market component will be the ultimate judge of the success or failure of the individual offerings.

One of the first mentions of the application of wargaming methodology in a business context appeared in 1958 in an article in the *Harvard Business Review* (Andlinger 1958). The terms used at the time were "business gaming" and "management simulation" and these tools were primarily used for training and education purposes, building on the experiences gained from military in wargaming. Andlinger broadly classifies wargames in two categories: "general" and "functional" games. General games aim to look at the company as a whole and focus on top management decisions determining the course of the enterprise, whilst functional games, as their name suggests, focus on particular functional areas of a company. Driven by specific questions from an operations research perspective, functional business wargames explore topics such as optimizing production, finance, or marketing efforts.

A year prior to the *Harvard Business Review* article, the American Management Association (AMA) was credited with the development of the first widely known business game, called *The AMA Top Management Decision Simulation* (Kalman and Rhenman 1975). The AMA game involved teams of players, representing the officers of different firms, making business decisions for their respective firm. Typically five teams, composed of three to five players each, had to decide on the production of a single product, which had to be sold in a competitive environment against the offerings of the other four teams. The simulation covered a time span of five to ten years of actual company operation and in order to make the computational burden for the participants bearable, the AMA game allowed each company team only a limited number of decision alternatives. A mathematical model, supported by limited computing power, was used to evaluate and calculate how the teams performed in relation to one another and what the likely outcome in the market place would be. Based on the success of the AMA game, a number of corporations and educational institutions in the US used the game and several new games were developed. The main focus of these early business games was on providing a learning experience, better preparing existing and potential managers for running a company.

During the next twenty or so years this focus did not really change until in the mid-1980s when wargaming was adapted towards business requirements in a more strategic context (Ginter and Rucks 1984; Treat *et al.* 1996). Initially used for education and training, business wargaming now focused on providing competitive intelligence, an activity primarily concerned with analyzing the competitors of a company, by better understanding the competition and their likely response to certain actions or inactions of a company in the market. More recently, the application of business wargaming has been expanded and now covers such areas as strategy formulation or validation of existing strategies (Kurtz 2003).

The global strategy and technology-consulting firm Booz Allen Hamilton was the first to establish a full-scale wargaming team, consisting of several ex-Navy and ex-military experts, who systematically developed the scope of possible business applications. The firm has conducted hundreds of simulations both in the US and around the globe, not only for businesses, but also for numerous governmental and non-profit organizations. The scope of their applications ranges from strategy formulation and validation to crisis response and enterprise resilience, visioning, and change management as well as the traditional education and training. Interestingly, over the course of the last few years, the firm has developed a scaled-down version of wargaming to be used in its recruiting efforts at top tier universities and business schools.

In the next chapter, we will take a closer look at the anatomy of a typical business wargame and highlight some of the key success factors for the successful setup of games as well as the extraction of the critical lessons learned to help significantly improve the way companies think about their market, their competitors and ultimately themselves.

Business Wargaming Methodology

2

The beginning is the most important part of the work.

To build upon the above quote from Greek philosopher Plato (*The Republic*, Book II, 377B), it is very important to be very clear and focused about what a wargame is set up for in the first place. The amount of preparatory work going into the development of a wargame depends on the type of simulation and the complexity of the questions to be answered. Among other factors, the amount of research, gamebook preparation, model development, duration of the simulation and need for professional coaching and moderation ultimately drive the overall cost of developing and running a wargame. In this chapter we will look at the mechanics of a typical wargame for strategy validation purposes. We are referring here to a business wargaming design which appears to be most commonly applied (e.g. Treat *et al*. 1996; Kurtz 2002, 2003). Other types of games, concerning design and purpose, will be explained in parts two and three, which will give a more complete overview of what it takes to design, prepare, execute, debrief and document a wargame.

What is Business Wargaming?

Before getting into the inner workings of a business wargame, we should spend some time to discuss what business wargaming is and what it is not. Many types of "games" exist and consequently there are a number of misconceptions about the process.

Let us start with what a business wargame is not. Business wargames are not your typical business school games. The kind of exercise in which you are asked to optimize the resources of a company by deciding how much you want to invest in advertising vs. production capacity or whether you should produce widgets type A instead of type B and at which price you will sell them. Such business school games, while admittedly useful in educational settings, are usually based on computer simulations with a set number of parameters, interlinked with pre-set sensitivities. Everyone who has ever participated in such a game will probably admit that after playing two or three iterations, they gathered a good sense for the sensitivities and an understanding on which parameters to focus on in order to maximize the results. The bottom line is that such games only have a finite number of lessons and, in the case of computer-based simulations, the answers are often built into the system. Their value for a top management team facing a difficult or disruptive situation or wanting to gain new insights into their business is virtually non-existent.

Rubel (2006) points out that computer simulations *per se* are not wargames; wargames require human players, maybe assisted by a computer. It can be argued that the kind of knowledge produced in computer simulation and the kind produced by a business wargame are different in nature. While a computer simulation appears not to produce new knowledge or insight (maybe the designing phase does), a role-playing simulation, like a business wargame, generates new knowledge through the social interaction of its participants (Fuller and Loogma 2007).

When we talk about business wargaming, we refer to a tailor-made simulation, which always starts with a blank sheet of paper; something that is entirely specific to a single organization that cannot be taken from firm to firm or sold over and over again. Each simulation is put together around a specific set of questions to which the business is seeking answers, such as:

- *Our industry is consolidating. Following several moves by competitors, there seem to be no good partners left. What should we do?* Prominent examples for these types of settings are the airline industry in the early 1990s, which moved quite suddenly from a competition of national carriers to a competition of alliances. Other examples would be the mega-mergers in the automotive, pharmaceutical or media industries, or the ongoing quest in almost any industry to find suitable acquisition targets that would ultimately create value and not add to the long list of failed integrations.

- *Is the business model in our industry changing? Does this mean that we will lose control over our market? Should we embrace new models, defend the status quo or both?* Examples here include the music industry and the threat from legal and illegal online models; the pharmaceutical industry and the threat from generic drugs; or incumbent telecommunications or energy providers in liberalized markets. Especially the recent discussions about environmental protection and whether and how sustainability aspects should be built into the way of doing business are other fields of application, e.g. when looking at the future of power trains in motor vehicles.

- *Is our industry/product becoming increasingly commoditized? If and how can we still make money? Should we close down and focus on alternative business opportunities?* Prominent examples here are the market for personal computers, mobile phone services, energy, or chemicals.

- *How resilient is our business? What happens if? Where is the next threat coming from? How much should we invest in countermeasures?* Questions like these have their roots in military scenarios, and yet they are increasingly important for businesses, industries and entire economies. Examples include more politically flavored simulations, such as how shifts in global power will develop, the impact of terrorist actions on economies, and also companies.

These are some of the main questions that can be addressed with wargaming. All of these situations are too complex to answer with conventional forms of analysis. Wargaming is a suitable means to explore them, because it combines elements of human decision making (and the inherent level of uncertainty) with a set of quantitative measures that allow you to gauge "what happens if." The methodology allows managers to test existing or newly conceived strategies in a dynamic, yet safe, environment. In doing so, they can save time, money and grief, gaining confidence in their plans via a relatively inexpensive simulation when compared to the cost of executing a potentially flawed strategy in the real world.

How Does Business Wargaming Work?—Teams

Any business wargame contains at least four elements: the company team, the competitor teams, the market team and the control team (Figure 2.1).

THE COMPANY TEAM

The company team represents the company conducting the wargame and aiming to answer the key strategic questions. The team is made up of senior managers from within the company and typically starts the game by executing its current strategic plan. In some instances, where a company deliberately wants to test alternative courses of action, the team may execute another hypothetical strategy or test an alternative business plan. In executing its strategy the team has all the liberty that it would have in the real world. It can form or dissolve alliances, conduct mergers and acquisitions or do anything else as long as it is within the boundaries of reality and within their resources.

THE COMPETITOR TEAMS

Like the company team, the competitor teams are staffed with senior managers from within the company. One interesting aspect is that these managers are forced to adopt the role of their own competitors and view their own company from this perspective. In order to facilitate the transition into their new role, they receive a copy of the so-called "gamebook," which gives them the most important facts about the company they are required to play as well as information on any other team. Coupled with the knowledge of their own company's weaknesses, they become formidable adversaries to the company team. Typically only the most significant competitors are represented by individual competitor teams. Smaller competitors are either consolidated into a group of competitors or represented by the control team.

THE MARKET TEAM

The market team represents the market participants and assumes the role of judging the relative attractiveness of all of the companies' offerings. This team is typically made up of market experts, who may come from within the client organization, may be external experts or, as is most often the case, may be a combination of the two. The market team forms a focus group that uses

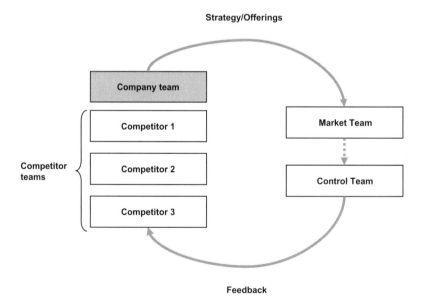

Figure 2.1   Elements of business wargaming

Source: Treat *et al.* 1996, 48

research, experience and intuition ultimately to award market shares. The team makes its call based on hard data, which is delivered by the competitor teams at specified times during the simulation, but also on the understanding of how well the message is communicated—the unique selling proposition (USP) of the respective teams in relation to one another and the rest of the market.

THE CONTROL TEAM

The control team "runs" the show. It is made up of wargaming experts, industry experts and typically the chief executive officer (CEO) or other senior executives from the company. Its first role is to structure and run the simulation, i.e. make sure that the schedule is adhered to, that the rules are observed and that presentations and feedback are given in the appropriate fashion and level of detail/structure. The team also calculates the quantitative variables based on the feedback from the market team and provides the company and competitor teams with the outcome, which typically includes the major positions of an income statement or cash flow. In some instances the control team will also introduce so-called "shocks," which are interventions to force the teams to address certain topics or go down a certain direction. In a product launch setting this could be the announcement of a product defect calling for a recall, or concerns that emerge about the safety of a product requiring some special approach to communication. Another very important function of the control team is to adopt the role of all other stakeholders not explicitly played in the simulation. Such stakeholders can be smaller competitors, regulators, or interest groups. The experts of the control team, faced with a proposed deal for an acquisition will take the role of the board of directors of the target company and decide whether they would accept the deal or not.

How does Business Wargaming Work?—Interaction

The above are the basic elements of a wargame. Now let's take a closer look at how these teams interact and how the simulation is actually played out.

A business wargame typically evolves over three moves, simulating a certain timeframe in real life (Figure 2.2). This timeframe can vary from a few months to several decades. The first move usually starts in the present and is based on all the available data at that time (i.e. now or any other determined point in time). A move is a decision cycle, which begins with the competing teams reviewing their strategy and taking their first actions towards an outcome. Such actions can be anything from launching new products or services out into the market, to forging alliances, investing in capacity or new markets, or

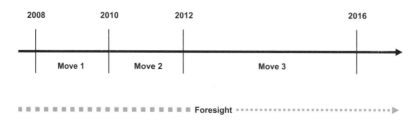

Figure 2.2   Example of an actual timeframe simulated over three game moves

running communication campaigns, such as communicating with the customer or lobbying other stakeholder groups. The decisions taken are documented in templates and provided to the market and control teams as hard data on which to base their decisions. In addition to this "input," the teams have the opportunity to present their offering in front of the market team (and everyone else in the market, e.g. competitor teams and the control team representing all other market participants as well). In this way—as in the real world—at certain points of the simulation, all parties involved have the same level of information on which they base their next steps.

The customers, played by the market team, will provide feedback and gauge the relative attractiveness of the various offerings by the company and competitor teams and award market shares. The control team then consolidates the hard data (such as price points, investments) and the soft data, in essence the perception of the market team/customers, in terms of what this would mean in numbers. The team calculates the overall size of the market, segment sizes, segment shares, profit margins etc. Due to the limited time and resources to run all the details, quantitative feedback will only include some key figures, e.g. of profit and loss statements, capital expense calculations or other key performance indicators (KPIs). The feedback from the control team represents the starting point for each team in the subsequent move. If, for example, one team "buys" market shares by dumping its products on the market for free, they most likely will make a major share gain in terms of new customers, but completely lose out on profitability. In this example, the team may find their choice of actions curtailed at the beginning of the second move as a result of lacking funds.

How does Business Wargaming Work?—Moves

A single move may take as long as a whole day. Figure 2.3 shows an overview of activity over the course of a simulation day.

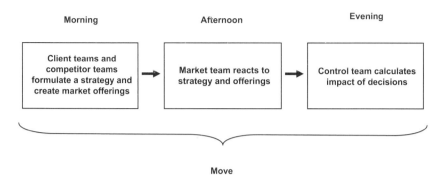

Figure 2.3   Overview of activities on a typical game day

Source: Oriesek and Friedrich 2003, 69

Typically in the morning the company and competitor teams will be analyzing the data and additional information available, prepare their offerings, strike deals, fill out templates and prepare their presentations for the plenary session around lunchtime. In the afternoon and evening the market and control teams get to work and calculate the market shares and quantitative impact, while the company and competitor teams are already working on their preparation for the next move. They continue to do so after they get the results from the market and control teams, and will adjust their preparation if necessary. Overnight, detailed results in the form of profit and loss statements and key data are calculated and reports are prepared as a starting point for the next move in the morning of the following day.

It is important that the teams, with exception of the plenary sessions, are separated and do not have any direct exchange with each other, e.g. by walking the hallways or visiting each other in their breakout rooms. All communication with competitors, alliance partners, acquisition targets etc. during the preparation phases must be channeled via email and by default always gets copied to the control team. The latter, as in the real world, will disseminate certain information, such as an agreed alliance between two competitors, to the other participants in order to make sure information equality is maintained. After all, such information will be disseminated via the media once a deal has been agreed upon. What may happen, however, is that the control team choose to pose some restrictions on a deal, for example, when anti-trust regulations would be violated or regulators would limit acquisitions to only parts of the business or impose the obligation to sell off other parts.

After all moves have been played out, a first assessment is made of what the lessons learned have been. The input is typically gathered in a plenary session during which participants reflect on what worked well in their strategies and what did not. The key insights from the game are gained from the mutual assessment of individual experiences focusing on the initial questions. In any case, after this initial assessment, a team of wargaming experts will dive deeper into the data gathered through the simulation and evaluates other sources such as the email traffic. The advantage of using email communication is that every message is logged and can be retrieved in the order in which it was sent out. Who was talking to whom about what can be traced. With this type of analysis trends or patterns can be identified, such as, for instance, when all players in the business wargame during a certain move aim to close similar types of acquisition or alliances. The detailed insights are usually consolidated in a report and presented about a week later to the sponsor of the game including recommendations for adjustments of the initial strategy.

The Relevance of Business Wargaming in Strategy

CHAPTER

3

There is a slightly odd notion in business today that things are moving so fast that strategy has become an obsolete idea ... that all you need is to be flexible or adaptable ... but if you do not develop a strategy of your own you become part of someone else's!

The above quotation from famous futurist and trend researcher Alvin Toffler (2000) captures some interesting aspects about strategy in today's context. The first half of the quotation reflects the general assumption that strategic planning is a long and inflexible process unable to cope with fast-changing environments. In the second part Toffler points to the fact that your ability to control your own future is entirely depending on the quality of your strategy. So, on the one hand, the world has become so complex that we are tempted to shift into a reactive mode, yet there is a desire for "hard data" and clear direction and therefore a multitude of management tools for dealing with complex and dynamic environments have been developed.

Bain & Company's annual survey of management tools (Rigby 2005) identifies strategic planning as the most popular and widely used tool in management. Grant (2003) concludes, drawing on his own study and on other recent evidence, that strategic planning continues to play a central role in the management systems of large companies, which of course has implications for strategic management.

Strategy and Tactics: A Military Point of View

Before we take a closer look at some tools for strategic planning, we should investigate in more detail what we mean when we talk about strategy. There is no commonly accepted definition for the terms "strategy," "strategic leadership" or "strategic planning." Of course there are many views and numerous books have been written about the topic, but whenever we have conducted wargaming workshops with business school students, or with experienced business people, we start the briefing session with the question: "What is strategy?" Usually after a few seconds of irritation and looks around the room, one participant raises his or her hand and says something like: "Strategy is necessary to reach the company's objectives." Other statements revolve around "Strategy is a game plan," "Strategy is the basis for sustained success" or "Strategy is obtaining and maintaining competitive advantage."

Strategy has served as a means to regulate the behaviour of groups, organizations and states in pursuing their vital interests, especially in the case of armed conflict. An interesting view on strategy, formulated by two retired military leaders, Lieutenant General (ret.) Josef Feldmann and Colonel (ret.) Paul Krüger (2007) of the Swiss Army, describes strategy as a bridge between where an organization stands today and where it wants to be tomorrow. In their view the pillars of the bridge are the values of the organization, which provide guidance for how this bridge is built between the now and the future. In this sense strategy (or the bridge) provides the directions for how to reach a certain vision or objective (see Figure 3.1).

If we simply look up "strategy" in the dictionary, we are likely to find a definition (Merriam-Webster's 1994, 1162) such as:

> *Strategy (Greek „strategia"), the science and art of military command exercised to meet the enemy in combat under advantageous conditions.*

In this sense, strategy refers to the deployment of troops. Based on information about the environment, e.g. in terms of terrain, light, weather, axes, settlements, waterways, as well as information about the enemy, e.g. in terms of size, strength, means at his disposal, location, timing, command and

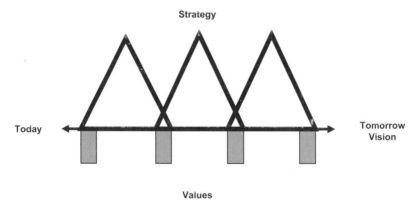

Figure 3.1   Strategy as a bridge

control structures, the military leader makes certain assumptions of where his adversary is most likely to strike, where he is most vulnerable and what is likely to happen next. Based on all this "hard" information and "soft" assumptions, as well as the knowledge about his own strengths and weaknesses, he will decide exactly how he wants to confront his adversary and where he wants his troops to be at the outset and during battle. In any case he will seek the most advantageous position in terms of his ability to develop impact on target. He will consider the factors of force, location, time and information to obtain an advantage over his enemy before actual contact.

Once the enemy has been engaged, attention shifts from strategy to tactics. Now, the deployment of troops is central. The strategic plan foresees a specific course of action, but its execution may be jeopardized by the enemy's response in terms of unexpected heavy resistance or unforeseen action. In such situations, the leader needs quickly to grasp the problem at hand and decide on an alternative course of action. If the leader is well prepared, he may be able to resort to prepared contingency plans, if not or in the case of complete surprise, he needs to improvise.

Although these explanations are military in nature, we believe that they are true in the business world as well. The means may not be as deadly, but the basics are the same. Through strategy we develop a game plan, watch over its execution and lead the actions of our organization and, yes, there are clearly situations where we need to improvise. Perhaps the simplest way to put it is when we say that strategy deals with three main questions:

1. What is the objective or vision you want to achieve with your business or organization?

2. What needs to be done to reach this objective? (game plan for execution/bridge)

3. What are the obstacles that may get in the way and what can you do about them?

The answer to question 3 should identify obstacles from within the company, from competitors, but also the larger environment such as legislation, stakeholder groups, technology and so on.

The Relevance of Strategic Planning and Scenario Planning

Figure 3.2 displays a typical strategic planning process, basically (1) setting objectives, (2) analyzing the environment and the company, possibly including scenarios and then (3) developing a set of strategic options, which if pursued, are refined to a level of detail which will allow for proper execution. Aside from finding answers to the three main questions, the important thing is that at the end of the process a strategic plan will always be chosen, which then is executed. But this is exactly where the greatest weakness of such a linear approach lies. By choosing a plan, the assumption is that after grinding all the data and collecting all available information, the plan is the single best answer and thus course of action to obtain the company objective. Strategic planning processes are a good way to understand past trends and allow extrapolation of these trends into likely future developments, but they are certainly not foolproof.

In a more sophisticated planning process the selection of the final plan may come after more or less elaborate scenario planning. The development of the scenario technique dates back to the 1950s when Herman Kahn of the RAND Corporation developed the first scenarios. In the 1970s Royal Dutch/Shell developed the scenario technique further into what is nowadays known as scenario planning, connecting the scenario technique with strategic planning. The main aim of scenarios is to identify existing trends and key uncertainties and combine them in pictures of the future, not as a means of covering all eventualities but in order to discover the boundaries of potential outcomes (Schoemaker 1992), cover generically different futures, and think about the unthinkable.

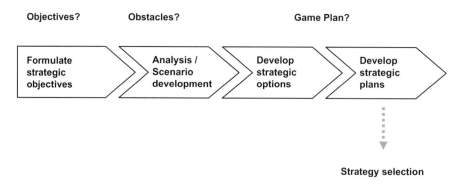

Figure 3.2   A typical strategic planning process

However, the former head of the scenario planning unit at Royal Dutch/Shell, Kees van der Heijden, points out that scenario planning actually developed out of military wargaming:

> As a strategic planning tool, scenario techniques are rooted in the military, where strategists have employed scenarios throughout history. Military organizations face considerable uncertainty in areas where decisions have to be taken fast and where the consequences are critical. They have used scenario planning, in an organizational context, in the form of what are known as 'war game' simulations. History has taught war leaders that preparation is crucial for success; war games improve the level of preparedness. (van der Heijden *et al.* 2002, 121)

Undoubtedly, scenario planning can help improve decision making, because it helps to think in alternatives; to assign probabilities to expected future outcomes and to formulate a comprehensive and cohesive strategy and even, ideally, contingency plans. Even with all these advantages scenario planning is still limited. This is because any scenario is fundamentally biased by the views of the person or people, who have developed the scenario in the first place and therefore is limited to the extent of their imagination. Furthermore, depending on the approach taken, scenarios can be nothing more than rational and safe extensions of the past and often classify likely outcomes along simple linear views of reality, whereas the real world involves complexity and multiple dimensions. While scenario planning is already a solid improvement of linear strategy development processes, nobel laureate Thomas Schelling hit the nail on the head when he supposedly said: "There is nothing harder to do than to come up with a list of all the things you have not thought about."

The Advantages of Business Wargaming

We are not saying that strategic planning processes or scenario planning are totally inadequate, but we know that by applying wargaming in the strategy definition process, we can test the strategic plan, whichever way it was originally put together, for its robustness under close to real-life conditions and thus significantly improve the outcome and reliability of the final strategic plan. We may also involve the participants, foster organizational learning (Senge 1990), and with luck challenge the mental models of those involved.

One of many advantages of business wargaming is the active involvement of participants. We in particular like the following quote from Paul Bracken (2001,

18), professor at the Yale School of Management, concerning the application of business wargaming in strategy formulation:

> *The problem with many strategy techniques is that they are too cold and bloodless. They fail to capture human emotions, and because of their icy rational character, people don't really pay attention to them. They are soon forgotten, and they make no lasting impact on the organization. Gaming is a profound learning experience, one that is not soon forgotten.*

During the course of a wargame the dynamics of a market and of the competitors will be analyzed, anticipated and experienced, by simulating a likely future over the course of several days. As a wargaming exercise evolves, the participants are exposed to creatively thinking about the future, which essentially will also expose them to some of the early signals of imminent change, which then may be relevant for the particular organization or the industry as a whole.

For business, as customary in the military, we are proposing that whenever time and resources permit, wargaming should be used to test a strategic plan before putting it into action and making significant investments. Van der Heijden (1998, 351) summarizes the relevance of testing a strategy in scenarios, which is also applicable for testing strategies by use of wargaming:

> *Strategy is the art of making choices—investing both for current and future success. To understand these choices clearly, organizations should identify a business idea and test it in substantially different scenarios. This process can help an organization to develop a business idea that will serve it well as the future evolves.*

The cost of a wargame, although not trivial, is far outweighed by the potential cost of a (wrong) decision made too quickly (and once made hard, to stop or reverse) and without exploring the full impact of a strategic plan. For example, if a company uses a wargame to test whether an intended acquisition will really lead to the expected synergies and advantages in the market that are assumed in the business plan, it may find out that it simply won't work and scraps the idea all together. In the case of a mobile network operator in Germany, who wanted to test its third generation mobile launch based on the then new UMTS (Universal Mobile Telecommunication System), in essence enabling mobile data, it helped them to pinpoint weaknesses in their original plan and better address otherwise underserved customer segments (the example is described in more detail in Chapter 4).

The history of military wargaming illustrates how wargaming was used by military planners throughout the centuries as a tool to cope with increasingly complex and dangerous environments and how the tool can be effectively applied in order to reduce the risks associated with strategic miscalculations (Ginter and Rucks 1984). Although business is not in all aspects equal to war, many of the same problems prevail and thus the application of wargaming and its potential benefits are significant.

Overall, the benefits of applying business wargaming can be summarized as follows:

- actively involves the participants;

- anticipates future developments in the simulation;

- multiple perspectives are included;

- multiple ways of learning;

- has team-building effects;

- provides a dynamic simulation.

Applications of Business Wargaming

Introduction

Part II is designed to provide you with an overview of the many applications of the business wargaming methodology. Bracken (2001) highlights, for instance , three types of wargames: technology integration games, path games, and shadow games. The purpose of the technology integration game is to find out in advance which obstacles may hinder the deployment of new IT systems, while the path game simulates a long period of time. The involved teams assess the moves of other teams and play restarts for another period. The objective is that the teams cannot start with a clean slate; rather they are exposed to their earlier decisions. Shadow games allow a senior executive to play out highly sensitive strategies without being involved, participating in the wargame indirectly, through an agent. Besides Bracken's view there are other categorizations (e.g. Bell 2003; Watman 2003). These mainly emphasize the relevance of wargaming for training and education and for the practise of all sorts of decision-making tasks. In addition, for instance, Vanderveer and Heasley (2005) emphasize the value of applying business wargames in the context of marketing.

Since this book is intended to provide a pragmatic introduction to business wargaming for practicing managers (and other interested parties), we have broadly categorized business wargames by fields of application. While this list may not be exhaustive, we believe the most important applications are:

- strategy testing
- crisis response preparation
- developing foresight
- change management
- training and recruiting
- some, as yet, undeveloped applications, such as reputation management and strategic early warning systems.

We have enclosed a good selection of real-life case studies; some of them well published others in part still confidential, to provide more insight into what business wargames can and cannot do. In order to honor confidentiality, not all the case studies can be discussed in the same level of detail. For the areas of reputation management and strategic early warning, we offer our view about how these applications might look like. In Chapter 10 a different view on designing a business wargame is offered.

We have structured each of the cases on the following basis:

- point of departure
- objectives and key questions
- game setup
- lessons learned.

Strategy Testing

CHAPTER

4

The most prominent application of business wargaming to date, clearly rooted in its primary military application, has been in the field of strategy testing. The idea is to take an existing strategic plan—which, as we have seen in Chapter 3, could have been developed in a simple or more elaborate form—and test it in a competitive environment in order to discover weaknesses, explore assumptions or simply find out whether it works or not. This may be projected into the future by simulating two to three strategic moves. Depending on the industry this may represent only a few months (technology-driven companies) or up to several years (more traditional process industries).

Why Strategy Testing?

One of the key challenges for today's managers is the formulation and execution of a strategy capable of adapting to the many complexities of a competitive environment and still generates value. Eden and Ackermann (1998) established that in most organizations the success of a strategy depends partly on its planning context. To ensure that a strategy is indeed robust, it should best be tested against a number of possible futures and include a number of options, which should mirror the context in which the organization is currently and will likely be operating going forward.

In the past scenarios have been perceived as being the preferred tool for strategy testing. Van der Heijden (1998) argues that the benefit of testing a strategy is to discover problems and difficulties well in advance of their becoming painfully evident. While we agree with this statement, we believe that wargaming has clear advantages over scenarios. Scenarios are limited by the imagination of their developers, who try to capture every aspect, yet are limited by what they know and what they can imagine as individuals. Whilst wargaming typically includes some likely scenarios, as hypotheses to be tested, they go one important step beyond the scenario in that they create an environment in which real people can explore all possibilities within the boundaries of reality and their imagination in order to reach their objectives. In this way, the scenario is no longer constrained by the brains of only the developers, but will develop iteratively, drawing on the actions and reactions of all participants and thus mirroring more closely what would happen in the real world where more than just the people in the strategy department are driving decisions.

Gilad (2004) states that business wargaming is the most effective managerial tool for assessing competitors' response to a changing industry. In his view, a wargame can help managers to predict their competitors' most likely moves. In this sense business wargames allow experimentation and learning with different strategies, without the risks of the significant cost of failure of the real world. By framing the scope and focus of the wargame early in the design phase, more or less emphasis can be placed on specific competitors, customers or other stakeholders. The trick is to narrow the focus down to a manageable set of constituents, which are then examined in detail rather than trying to simulate everything. Done well, a wargame can offer invaluable insights into customer and competitor behaviors and other relevant developments which would otherwise go unnoticed. The inclusive experience, which offers a CEO or a company the opportunity for many top managers to learn the lessons for themselves, is of significant benefit. After all, insight gained via personal experience far outweighs pre-packaged conventional wisdom whether presented in a business book, a course or by a consultant.

These are the benefits of a dynamic team approach:

- uncovers weaknesses in the original strategic plan;

- provides better understanding of competitors and their possible actions;

- encourages participants to think creatively about the future and thus overcome organizational blindness and revitalize the thinking about their own business;

- teaches participants to learn to trust their own strategy, because they have seen what works and what doesn't;

- sharpens awareness amongst participants of the wider environment, team dynamics and the issues critical to the success of their own business.

These aspects which make the case for business wargaming are reflected in the following three case studies. The first case example describes an airline company in the late 1990s struggling, in common with many of its competitors, to find answers as to how to best deal with the dramatic developments in its industry.

The second case study explores the experience of a European mobile operator, faced with the dilemma of introducing new service offerings following the decision to invest heavily in a new technology. How might they enter the market to recoup their investment and what were competitors likely to do?

The third case study illustrates briefly how the General Staff College in Switzerland uses wargaming to test the robustness of concepts of operations.

Case Study: Alliance Strategy for Airlines[1]

This wargame was run with a leading European airline, desperately looking for answers to complexity in its environment and seeking reassurance that it was doing the right thing. The aim was to test the viability of the current strategy, in particular in the light of how to position itself within the context of global alliances.

POINT OF DEPARTURE

During the 1970s Open Skies legislation was introduced in the US, which led to deregulation and greater competition not only in the US, but also in Europe and much of the rest of the world. The European Economic Area and later the European Union adopted a system of free connectivity between destinations in its territory which meant the competition on many routes grew significantly, dropping prices and squeezing profits. With lower prices airfares had become affordable to a wider group of customers who increasingly viewed air travel as a commodity to buy on the basis of lowest price. In this environment, the common strategy for airlines was to forge alliances, such as Star Alliance or One World, in order (a) to lock customers in by providing them with a wider network through which they might reach more destinations without having to go outside of the alliance and (b) because it allowed them to realize economies of scale, including co-sharing flights, thus increasing seat load factors; as well as realizing benefits in other areas such as maintenance, purchasing, training and so on. During this period competition gradually shifted from the level of

---

1   Information taken from a public speech by George E. Thibault, then Principal with Booz Allen
    Hamilton, at the Swiss General Staff College, 2001, and Lüchinger (2001).

national airlines to that of alliances as airline mega-merges were prohibited by regulators.

The central strategic question for many airlines, including the one that commissioned the game of this case study was: should they join one of the existing alliances, stay independent or even be so bold as to lead the formation of a new alliance? Further questions explored whether the airline would be strong enough to survive outside the existing alliances; what would happen to its negotiating influence with any alliance the longer it postponed the decision; and how might the business model and the economics within the airline industry be likely to change in the future?

Conventional methods, such as market analysis and scenario planning tools, were perceived as inadequate for fully exploring the forces in the market and no united view existed within the firm as to how best handle the challenges. As a result the airline decided to commission consulting firm Booz Allen Hamilton to run a wargame with them and find the answers to its many questions.

OBJECTIVES AND KEY QUESTIONS

After a series of in-depth interviews with top client representatives, the following objective and key questions were identified: provide and train the top management team with insights on how to think about the future of the airline business and how best to position the company in order to compete successfully in the changing environment. More specifically:

- Can the airline succeed with its current strategy in Europe and the rest of the world?

- To what extent might the airline realistically operate outside any major alliance? Failing that, whom should it ideally link up with and what was its bargaining position?

- Which are the most important markets and client segments?

- How should a national airline position itself versus regional and global competitors?

- How should the network, fleet and capacity be organized?

- Is the current distribution model still sufficiently robust to succeed in this environment?

GAME SETUP

The overall preparation for the game took about three months, in order to assemble the necessary information, decide on the setup and structure and the game process. The final setup comprised six teams (see Figure 4.1), including the client airline, five competitor teams, three of which focused on existing alliances with the respective lead airline and two which represented airlines in a similar situation as the client. The setup also included a market and a control team. The market team represented various customer segments whilst the control team, besides structuring the simulation, also assumed the role of the regulators and all other players, which were not explicitly played as part of the competitor teams. The wargame was played out in three moves, each covering a three-year period, from 1999 to 2008.

The game opened with the situation as it presented itself in 1999. This was characterized by talks between airlines about alliances, US and Asian airlines in particular, as well as an exploration of anti-trust issues between American and European partners, which would allow for alliances, but would not allow mergers and takeovers. The regulatory environment remained stable for moves

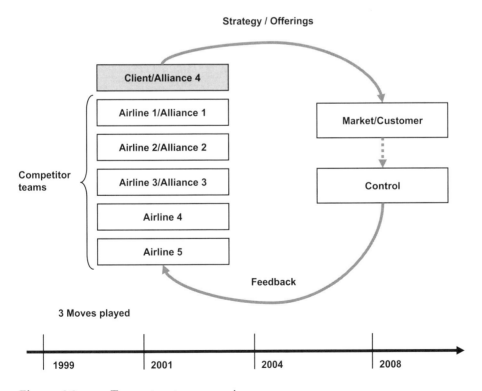

Figure 4.1   Team structure overview

one and two and was then significantly relaxed for move three to reflect the pattern of other industries. Now mergers, including transcontinental ones, would be allowed and anti-trust immunity was no longer granted.

And so on one fine morning in March of 1999, the CEO and approximately 50 of his top managers, as well as a group of airline and wargaming experts, and support staff, gathered at the airline's headquarters. The managers had previously received reading briefings to familiarize themselves with the roles they were to play over the course of the next three days. The day opened with a briefing session:

- providing an overview of the situation at the start of move one;

- setting the objectives for the simulation; and

- dividing the teams up.

The plenary session was then adjourned and the teams retreated into their syndicate rooms, each accompanied by an experienced partner from the consulting firm in the role of coach.

Within the team rooms, materials were studied, conclusions were drawn, strategies formulated and, inquiries for alliances or other forms of partnerships were exchanged using an email set up between the teams, and questions were directed to the control team. Using email as the only means of communication enabled negotiations to be kept secret until they were revealed to the public, which either happened in the subsequent plenary session, where every team had to lay open their plan for the next move or for dissemination through the control team.

The teams faced clear set schedules and deadlines within which to complete their strategies, which had to be formulated in a set of templates to ensure consistency and comparable information between the strategies compiled by the different teams. Throughout the simulation one major hurdle remained. Participants were required to challenge and overcome their current mental models about their company and the industry. This was not particularly easy as their own CEO had already fixed in his own mind the strategic option he wanted to pursue. The uncertainty of outcome created throughout the simulation was one aspect of the process that he and the management teams found particularly hard to accommodate.

LESSONS LEARNED

There were plenty of lessons from this wargame. To summarize the most important:

1. The realization that any existence outside of a major alliance would be increasingly difficult. As suspected, the network effects, operational efficiencies and potential cost savings from the economies of scale put tremendous pressure on national airlines who were too little to be global players and too big to be niche players.

2. The bargaining power of any airline wanting to join a major alliance would decrease the longer it hesitated. The network of the alliances was becoming more and more dense over time which meant the value added by any new member would tend to decrease and that alliances would become more powerful as they attracted more candidates with the ability to pick and choose their partners. With a good network coverage, alliances would now shift from increasing the network by adding new partners to deepening the integration of the existing partners.

3. The understanding that customers would continue to demand cheaper fares, better coverage and become increasingly more powerful. With so many players out there trying to fill their seats and competing on price (with the exclusion of select niche players) the market had fundamentally shifted from a cost plus model, in which airlines had basically dictated prices for tickets, to a model where customers would indicate what they were willing to pay and airlines would try to offer the flight while still making a profit.

4. The transatlantic routes had most passengers and were the fastest-growing and most profitable routes in the world. To do business on these routes required the ability to feed passengers onto the transatlantic flights, which was also a driver for controlling the home market. For this particular client, at the time, Asia did not have the strategic importance that was generally assumed.

5. Global alliances had already been more or less established and would not change dramatically going forward. These alliances would increasingly move to a mode of co-existence rather than fierce competition, which would help stop the price erosion.

6. With the loosening of regulatory restrictions would come a new compulsion to adopt a model of even deeper integration by means

of mergers and acquisitions across borders All the players needed to be prepared, should regulation change.

As mentioned earlier the CEO was sold on a particular course of action, which revolved around the formation of a fourth alliance. While basically a valid option, the question remained whether this would really make sense—given the remaining candidates for this alliance were in the main often poorly operated and weakly positioned—or whether it would be smarter to just join an existing alliance. The CEO chose to stick with his conviction that the former was the better option and after thanking the consultants decided to do just that and after thanking the consultants decided to do just that (Lüchinger 2001).

He continued to establish a new alliance with participation of several partners of questionable value which substantially eroded the cash base of the client over the years without ever reaping the benefits from a successful network of companies. Over time the company became so cash constrained that it went bankrupt, the alliance was dissolved and parts of the assets were carried over into a new company, which finally joined one of the formerly existing alliances relatively recently.

There is no suggestion that wargaming in its own right would have prevented this outcome, but at least at the time it provided solid indications that developing their own alliance with the partners still available would prove to be extremely difficult and should at least have been re-examined thoroughly.

Case Study: 3G Mobile Data Market Entry[2]

Having paid an enormous amount in the auction for one of the third generation (3G) mobile telephony licenses in Europe and agreeing to invest a similar amount into building up the respective infrastructure as a condition to obtain the license in the first place, a large European mobile operator wanted to examine whether its current market entry strategy was the right one or if it needed to be adjusted.

POINT OF DEPARTURE

In 2000 a number of European countries were auctioning off the third generation (3G/UMTS) mobile licenses to interested mobile network operators (MNOs). The so called "3G standard," also known as UMTS, has the advantage over the second generation (2G) mobile technology that it provides a higher speed for

---

2   Information taken from Oriesek and Friedrich (2003) and from participant interviews.

data transmission thus enabling the use of complex multimedia applications. Depending on whether you are stationary or on the move, the transmission rate for data can reach as high as 2 Mbit/s and thus basically provides broadband access on the go, which in turn enhances the potential uses of cell phones or similar mobile devices to include surfing the web at reasonable speeds, e-commerce, multimedia applications, video broadcastings, video conferencing and so on.

Based primarily on the decision by MNOs to secure access to this promising new technology, in Germany at total of six UMTS licenses were auctioned off in a fierce bidding war and ultimately representing a tax revenue of about $45 billion to the government. This auction forced the MNOs to assume tremendous levels of debt, leading experts and financial analysts to express doubts about the probable success of 3G and whether it would ever recover the sunk cost. Whilst there was no shortage of ideas for potential applications at the time, no one knew what the killer applications of the future could or would be.

The wargame was facilitated for a large mobile network operator and the client company had already developed a market entry strategy for mobile data, enabled by UMTS. However, a far-sighted executive realized that conducting a wargame, especially in light of the substantial additional investments in marketing, product development and other related costs, would probably make sense to focus the strategy more effectively or at least gain the confidence that this was indeed the right way to go.

OBJECTIVES AND QUESTIONS

The objective of the wargame was to stress test the existing market entry strategy especially with respect to potential market developments and competitor actions, and to uncover any issues or opportunities previously not reflected in the strategic plan. More specifically:

- Was the company focusing on the right customer segments?

- Were the assumptions relating to the attractiveness of specific mobile data offerings for specific customer segments correct? If not – why and could anything be done to change them?

- Would the market accept the proposed pricing models as planned by the company?

- Were the chosen distribution channels suitable for the rollout and did the market value the planned customer service offerings?

- Would it make sense to acquire a second license?

- Would the planned content strategy involving selected partners be sufficient to differentiate the operator in the market?

- Were the measures to overcome technical hurdles (availability of handsets, network coverage, handover and so on) sufficient and how vulnerable would the offering be to substitution (WLAN, value-added GSM offerings)?

- Was the envisioned schedule appropriate?

GAME SETUP

A total of six competitor teams were planned at the outset of the game, but this was consequently reduced to four main competitors as some of the initial competitors either went out of business or decided not to roll out the UMTS technology. A market and a control team were used to structure and control the game and represent all other constituents in the market. The competitor teams, including the client team, consisted of a team leader, a team briefer, a team communicator, and a business wargaming expert in the role of coach.

The main task of the team leader was to lead the discussion and make sure that the essential issues were covered. The team briefer was responsible for creating the slides for the plenary sessions. The team communicator operated the email communication between the teams and the control team. The expert coach supported the team leader, making sure the timelines and templates were followed and that the teams stayed on track and ensuring a more or less consistent level of quality for the plenary sessions. If necessary the coach would also act as devil's advocate and pose open questions to steer the teams back on track if they diverted onto tangents.

As in the airline example, prior to the wargame, each participant received a copy of the gamebook consisting of information such as profiles for each company played, market trends, financials, market research and so on. The gamebook comprised the basic set of background information that would be the same for all participants at the outset of the game. Its contents were compiled using public information from annual reports, news clippings, analyst reports and other sources. Broadly the gamebook would cover market information and provide a structured profile for each competitor team including broad and more specific mobile strategy, financial and market performance, business activities, service offerings, distribution channels and competitive strengths and weaknesses.

The wargame was played out over three moves, played on three days. The moves were structured along a strategic decision cycle, so move one simulated the first year or the "market entry," move two simulated the second year and how the company positioned its offering versus the competitors in its effort to solidify its position and market share, and the third move looked further forward, simulating two to three years in the future, in order to explore how things would play out following move two and how positions would solidify in the long run.

The objective for the four competitor teams was to develop and implement a strategy for launching mobile data services that leveraged 3G technologies. The strategy comprised detailed action plans with clear decisions about pricing, product or service design, marketing and promotion as well as distribution. On top of these basic decisions, the teams also had to quantify their courses of actions in terms of detailed quantitative statements covering operating costs and capital expenditures. They did so using templates provided by the control team.

The teams were allowed to communicate with each other and the broader market, but again only via email and by simultaneously informing the control team. The members of the market team started by refining a clear set of customer preferences, weighted by customer segment. This would serve them as a basis for evaluating the competitor teams' offerings in the plenary sessions and rank their appeal in order to determine the likely changes in market share.

They would do so by using scoring sheets, which could then be input into the market model run by the control team. Besides running the model, the control team's responsibilities also included keeping all teams equally informed about external events and major developments resulting from competitor actions. This team also represented the government regulators, board of directors and any other entities, whose roles could not be played explicitly during the game, but were needed to give approval of actions, make board decisions etc.

In terms of the market model and financial impact, the simulation started with the financials, subscriber numbers, churn rates, margins, products, and distribution networks as they existed in real life for each of the competitor teams. The first move was dominated by partnerships to set up fixed-mobile bundles and a strong focus on acquiring content that could be offered on new mobile platforms. In this situation the large players, who in some instances were part of a larger telecoms group, which already offered online services through their internet platforms, were at an advantage, but took some time to establish the influence such a leveraging of in-house capabilities would carry. The smaller players tried hard to strike attractive content deals, but found themselves often constrained by the financial resources they were able to commit to such strategies. In any case, gaining exclusivity on content deals proved to be very expensive and thus differentiation had to be driven by other levers as well.

During move two, the large players continued to leverage their inhouse capabilities whilst customers appeared to adapt to the new offerings less quickly than hoped for. This was in part because, aside from the early adopters, the general public needed more time and most importantly education on the new services, headsets and what the value added would be for them. This triggered a number of creative approaches to the distribution channels, i.e. assistance educating customers in switching from 2G to 3G offerings.

During the final move, the teams pretty much continued their approach and tried to optimize their position on the basis of what they perceived to be working or not in the market. Consequently, the teams were largely concerned with focusing on DSL/UMTS bundles, further marketing UMTS and engaging in strong partnerships which focused on the corporate market, which seemed to be less price sensitive and more receptive for the new services. One thing was striking and remained unchanged each time the simulation was played: no clear killer application emerged that would significantly drive the adoption of mobile data services and that would allow the players to generate the huge cash flow needed to quickly recoup the investments made.

LESSONS LEARNED

The lessons learned from this business wargame can be broken down in three areas:

- strategy
- sales and marketing and
- communication.

Strategy   The wargame revealed that the large-scale players able to use group synergies between their fixed line and online business could leverage assets onto mobile platforms. The two large-scale players in particular started out very cautiously, focusing on defending market shares at the expense of innovation. Consequently, they lacked a clearly differentiated position and , although they enjoyed a cost and synergy advantage, their offerings did not really shape the market nor drive the future of mobile data.

The two smaller players, on the other hand, well aware that they had to be innovative, had considerably more risk appetite and would try out some wacky scenarios even if the outcomes were not always sure. In some instances these did not work and in other instances they worked extremely well. After some delay, the large-scale players tried to copy some of the good ideas developed by the smaller players and aimed at doing so with greater efficiency. This had the effect of forcing the smaller players to reinvent themselves constantly in order to stay ahead of the curve and in an effort to develop a loyal (for example, community-based) customer base.

Another strategic theme that emerged was the significance of being able to provide an international footprint. The corporate sector, in particular, appreciated the availability of services wherever their travel would take them. Good content, driven by handsets that could display it in a user-friendly fashion and powered by a reliable high-speed network could also drive customer usage, especially in the case of high-data volume applications, such as streaming audio and video. For some of the smaller players, a plain vanilla low-cost strategy seemed to work out equally well. The team developed this as far as limiting their offering only to selling SIM cards and pre-paid cards via distribution partnerships.

Sales and Marketing With regards to sales and marketing, the following themes emerged: for one the quality (highly trained sales reps, prime locations, availability etc.) of sales channels would be key in bringing complex data products to the subscriber as such offerings would involve an element of educating the customer in how to effectively use the service. Derived from this the proliferation of "low care," almost self-service sales channels seemed very unlikely and not worth pursuing. It also turned out that exclusivity of sales channels (e.g. company-owned stores vs. shelf space with distributors) would further determine how much control and thus success the company would have in bringing its products to the end user. Last but not least, it became clear that the new offerings would need a significant "marketing push" in close coordination with a powerful sales organization because of the aforementioned specificities of successfully selling the product/service, but also because it was not exactly a situation where the market had just been waiting to absorb the product.

Communication It became obvious that companies would be better off concentrating their efforts on marketing one or two select mobile data applications (i.e. MMS, mobile portals) rather than trying to market everything at once with the same intensity. The game also revealed that a constant effort must be undertaken in order to communicate the "value" of mobile data offerings to the end user if demand was not to remain low.

Further Lessons Learned In terms of customer segments, the corporate market proved to be most receptive to value-added services. Further lessons learned involved pricing, where flat fee structures and simplicity of plans seemed to trump complex per unit models. Handset design and functionality also emerged as a key success factor in driving the adoption of the new technology.

At a macro level, the fit of the new service offerings in the overall product/service portfolio of the company proved to be important as well. For example, the launch of single creative products/services was perceived as essential, but this would be difficult to sell to the youth segment if the overall company were more associated with business customers or older consumers.

These are some of the general lessons that could be learned from the game. The specific lessons for the client remain confidential and therefore cannot be elaborated in detail. However, the insights from this game allowed the client to refine its initial strategic plan and make valuable adjustments, e.g. by refocusing on the appropriate market segments with a targeted offering that would help reduce overall cost and lead to higher adoption rates.

In a Nutshell: Business Wargaming in the Swiss General Staff College

As in many other nations, the Swiss General Staff College teaches an introduction to wargaming as part of their curriculum. The aim is that students learn how to validate the concepts, which they developed during practicing the action planning process, via means of wargaming.

Under the leadership of the chief of staff the officers are divided up into different teams. One team plays the enemy (red) and the other team plays friendly troops (blue). Allowing time for action and reaction, the participants move tank battalions, infantry units, heavy artillery and other units step-by-step across the battlefield, which is represented by a giant map. Done correctly the game provides valuable insights about the validity of the assumptions behind each of the movement decisions. Will the enemy use the routes that we anticipated? Will logistics work, once our forward elements are so far ahead? Can air defense elements keep up and ensure freedom of movement? What happens if we lose all or part of our artillery in a counter-battery shoot out?

What are the critical elements that need to be synchronized during an attack or defensive action?

The wargaming can take anywhere from a few hours up to a few days. Depending on the depth and complexity of the debriefing, the insights can lead to major changes that will eventually find their way back into the action plans. While the methodology will basically work at any level of unit from battalion up, because of the intensive preparation, manpower needed and effort needed to run it, it is more appropriate for larger units of brigade size and above.

Crisis Response Preparation

A second common application of wargaming is crisis response preparation. In this chapter we will look at three case studies. The first case deals with a provider of financial information services that wanted to test out what would happen in the case of a terrorist attack. The findings are for the largest part confidential, nevertheless we would like to highlight some of the general conclusions relevant to the topic of crisis response.

This is followed by a well-publicized wargame, conducted at the national level, in India and several other countries, with the objective of exploring scenarios around the proliferation of HIV (Human Immunodeficiency Virus)/ AIDS (Acquired Immune Deficiency Syndrome) and the likely impact of countermeasures designed to contain the problem before it became a major national crisis; with all the associated impact on the population, the economy, national health systems and so on.

The third case study, which was also well publicized and conducted at a national level, focuses on the wargame that was run for the US government shortly after 9/11. The game examined a likely scenario for a bioterrorism attack and explored how well prepared the country was, and what further action was needed to respond more effectively going forward. Before diving into the case studies, we will briefly cover the implications business wargames can have for crisis management.

Implications of Business Wargames for Crises Management

The value of wargaming has been recognized in particular for crisis preparation (McCown 2005). Crises have become an inevitable, natural feature of our daily lives. They are no longer an aberrant, rare, random, or peripheral feature of business. Crises do not happen because a single part of a complex system fails, they occur because a significant amount of the overall systems fails (Mitroff

2000). The paradox associated with crisis management is described by Mitroff, Pearson and Harrington (1996, 59):

> *We cannot understand fully what we need to do during crises unless we first understand what we need to do and have in place before a crisis; at the same time, we can not understand fully what we need to do beforehand unless we understand what we will be required to do during a crisis.*

Business wargames can help resolve the paradox. As the cases studies will illustrate, a wargame allows the participants to actually experience how they themselves or their organization are prepared to deal with crises. Mitroff *et al.* (1996) further point out that an important part of effective crisis management involves training exercises and simulations, which can also be achieved through a business wargame as a strategic simulation.

A wargame can also be helpful in identifying the strengths and weaknesses of organizations in dealing with crises; analyzing the crisis response capabilities of an organization by conducting a crises management audit (Mitroff *et al.* 1996), in contrast to the participative wargame.

A wide range of studies on crises suggest that they occur because of a breakdown in the links between organizations, people, and technologies. The number of organizations and people caught up in a crisis can be significant which means that it is important to expand the number of relevant stakeholders, beyond the most immediate group of employees, managers, and unions (Mitroff *et al.* 1996). As mentioned before, any crisis results from one or more critical points in any system either failing or operating at reduced capacity. While crises themselves can never be fully prevented, several levers exist to minimize the risk or impact by reducing the likelihood that events occur in the first place or that one or more events will cause a crisis and by improving the reaction in case your organization faces a state of pre-crisis or full crisis.

Good preparation is the key to both and can be achieved on the one hand by improving the system itself; building in redundancies or taking measures to improve the critical points within the system, and on the other hand by establishing and embedding procedures that will help reduce reaction time and deliver results quickly.

The value of applying wargames in preparation for managing in a crisis lies primarily in the opportunity to understand complex systems better in order to see where the critical points lie and what other problems may cause or exacerbate a potential crisis, such as blockades in the exchange of information between key constituents. Wargaming will also allow you to test for scenarios that are likely and yet include events that you might not have thought of or that were not recognized for the potentially fatal impact they could have on the system. Preparing for the expected, but more importantly for the unexpected, is the key objective to keep in mind when wargaming for crisis response preparation.

The following case studies show the value of wargames in helping the participants to understand the importance of working together with multiple stakeholders to resolve crises and establish partnerships between several different sectors.

Case Study: Financial Information Provider

POINT OF DEPARTURE

After 9/11 many businesses were worried and asked themselves how vulnerable their operations were to terrorist attacks. One such business was a large provider of financial information and transaction-related data for the exchanges between central banks, high street banks and clearing institutions. The CEO wisely decided to run a series of wargames to understand better the vulnerabilities of his business and to enable his top management to understand these vulnerabilities and train its crisis response organization in dealing with the problem.

OBJECTIVES AND QUESTIONS

- What would happen to the infrastructure and ability to provide services in case of terrorist attacks?

- How effective would the crisis response team be in dealing with the situation?

- How could the company best manage the effects such attacks have on their customers?

- What were the technical consequences in case of multiple event scenarios?

GAME SETUP

While the details remain confidential, the setup consisted of a number of customer teams (central and high street banks) in different locations all dependent on the services of the client, plus a client team and the control team running the simulation. A number of technical experts were involved to examine the exact implications various incidents would have on the technical infrastructure and what this would mean in terms of maintaining services for the clients, likely down times and so on.

The initial scenario involved a terrorist attack on one of the company's global data centers. The common belief at the time was that while an attack of this kind might cause some delays in service delivery, the effect could quickly be mitigated by switching capacity to a redundant "hot site," where servers would be up and running and could take over the load from the affected data center almost instantaneously.

During the simulation, however, the control team expanded the scenario to include a second and further attacks on other data centers, which would seriously reduce the capacity of the system to deliver service up to the point where the company had to fire up an additional "cold site" in which servers were in place, but where applications and data needed to be brought up to speed. The consequences would be serious delays in services and significant non-availability of systems.

The way the game was played out, the attacks occurred locally and the company was unaware of them until reports from the media or phone calls from local clients enquiring why services were not available started coming in. This posed the first challenge to the client: how to find out what had happened and get a complete view of the situation and when and how to trigger the crisis response team.

In the subsequent steps the teams were required to execute emergency plans, in close cooperation with the technical experts and the management of the company. As more and more attacks were reported, a strategy was needed to communicate with customers, employees, the media and to prioritize data traffic, focusing on the high priority items only while backlogging everything else for execution once the system capacity would allow to do so.

LESSONS LEARNED

The first lesson was that no matter how well prepared you think you are, you can always be better prepared!

While the client had a designated crisis response team and had also taken certain technical precautions to prevent serious problems with its service delivery, the main area for improvement lay in the execution of the process. This included, firstly, how to find out that there is a problem fast; secondly, how to gain a speedy picture of the full extent of the problem; thirdly, how to put into gear the necessary contingency plans; and, finally and most importantly of all, how to communicate openly and clearly with customers and other constituents. This communication would need to contain detailed instructions on how to prioritize data traffic according to importance as well as the ability to make fairly accurate predictions as to when the backlog would be worked off and the infrastructure would be running at full capacity again.

While many of these steps may appear commonsensical, the company found significant room for improvement in execution. And since there is no opportunity to test systems with a real crisis, wargaming offered a very effective means of practicing procedures in as close a manner to the real thing as possible. In the case of this particular client, the wargame helped them become faster, better coordinated and technically better prepared for the possibility of multiple events; something inconceivable before 9/11, because previous plans assumed only single incidents. As recent history has shown, terrorist attacks that have consisted of concerted multiple site events that in their combination trigger a far greater crisis are more common then previously suspected.

Case Study: HIV/AIDS[1]

In October of 2003, a collaborative team consisting of consulting firm Booz Allen Hamilton, the Global Business Coalition under Richard Holbrook, and the Confederation of Indian Industry conducted a business wargame in New Delhi. The game, which looked at the HIV/AIDS epidemic in India, explored what would happen if nothing were done to mitigate the epidemic and sought to stimulate creative thinking across stakeholders on how the problem could be solved or at least contained.

---

1   Information taken from Booz Allen Hamilton (2004).

POINT OF DEPARTURE

According to India's National AIDS Control Organization, in 2002 there were between 3.82 and 4.52 million HIV/AIDS cases in the country. At that time the primary route of infection (approximately 85 percent) was heterosexual exposure. The prevalence of HIV/AIDS was high and rising with certain groups, such as intravenous drug users and homosexuals, at particularly high risk. Mobile workers, meaning workers traveling through the country from job to job, effectively constituted the bridge between the high-risk groups and the general population, fuelling the rapid spread of the disease. During this process the disease increasingly moved out of the urban centers into the rural communities, millions of people would have contracted the disease and the expected GDP loss for the Indian economy would be enormous. Based on this scenario, all participating constituents realized that something needed to be done.

OBJECTIVES AND QUESTIONS

Using this grim scenario, the goal of the wargame was to stimulate a creative collaboration between multiple constituents and show how their actions would potentially alter the scenario—what might prove to be effective (or not). Based on these insights, specific recommendations and action plans could be put to work to prevent the uncontrolled spread of the disease that threatened to cost many lives and seriously damage India's economy. The participants focused on five key objectives (Booz Allen Hamilton 2004: 2):

1. "Develop a better understanding of the long-term economic, political, and social impacts of HIV/AIDS.

2. Understand the impact of potential interventions.

3. Identify areas for collaboration between the public and private sectors.

4. Determine how best to mobilize both business and public sector resources.

5. Identify strategies for all sectors in developing a national HIV/AIDS response."

GAME SETUP

The two-day event was jointly developed and hosted by Booz Allen Hamilton, the Global Business Coalition on HIV/AIDS (GBC), and the Confederation of Indian Industry (CII).

GBC includes over 200 companies worldwide, aiming at meeting the challenges of the HIV/AIDS pandemic through access to the skills and expertise of the business sectors. The GBC helps each individual member company to develop a business plan or strategy for their HIV/AIDS response. In addition, through its partnerships with non-governmental organizations (NGOs), governments and civil society, the GBC encourages member companies to apply their core competencies and products to the response to HIV/AIDS.

The CII is a non-government, not-for-profit industry-led and -managed organization. It is India's premier business association, with a direct membership of over 6,000 organizations from the private as well as public sectors, with an indirect membership of over 98,000 companies from around 342 national and regional sectoral associations. The aim of the CII is to create and sustain an environment conducive to the growth of industry in India, partnering industry and government alike through advisory and consultative processes.

Overall more than 200 leaders from industry, government, healthcare and community organizations and NGOs participated. Business participants included senior executives from industries including consumer products, financial services, heavy manufacturing, information technology, pharmaceuticals, automotive, and energy. Representing the government were national and state officials from India, as well as officials from the US, the United Kingdom, Germany, and Australia. Civil society leaders from international organizations including UNAIDS, Global Fund, Oxfam, Gates Foundation, Gere Foundation, World Bank, and the World Economic Forum were also in attendance. Participants also included leaders from domestic NGOs such as Action India AIDS Project, Family Planning Association of India, India HIV/AIDS Alliance, and Sahara.

Booz Allen Hamilton developed an approach to the wargame which included an analytical framework at its core and which leveraged epidemiological and economic modeling and partnerships with leading academic centers. The completed model, which incorporated as many as 1,000 variables, offered a new means of quantifying the proliferation of the disease and more importantly also the impact actions taken by the public and private stakeholders would have on this proliferation by altering one or a series of these variables. The wargame was played over three moves, simulating 10 years into the future.

As depicted in Figure 5.1 a multitude of stakeholders were involved in the wargame. The participants were divided into nine teams representing industry, government, and civil society, with a mix of sector representatives assigned to each team. This allowed individuals to share their insights and knowledge, providing all participants with a broader perspective of the impact of the disease and the consequences of HIV/AIDS interventions and policies. In addition, a facilitation team from Booz Allen Hamilton oversaw the wargame.

The highly interactive exercise allowed the teams to communicate with each other via email, in order to seek information, assistance, and funding, and to form partnerships. The epidemic evolved according to the actions taken by the teams. Over a series of three moves a span of ten years was simulated, forcing the participants to address real-world dilemmas, and manage the short- and long-term consequences of their action.

Over the course of the wargame the teams experienced the consequences of relying on broad prevention and the education programs as the disease spread rapidly to the middle class. They dealt with the challenges of funding constraints as they developed programs that ended up not being implemented due to lack of resources. During the wargame the participants were faced with pressure and constraints similar to those in the real world. Not only were they required to propose effective interventions but also to develop strategies that could actually be implemented. They quickly discovered that no single sector would be able to tackle HIV/AIDS without leveraging the knowledge, talents,

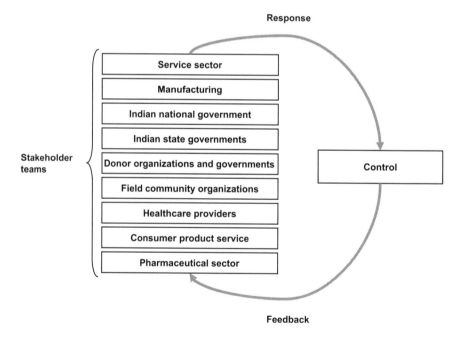

Figure 5.1   Team structure overview

and resources of others. Developing effective partnerships among diverse groups of stakeholders presented several challenges (Booz Allen Hamilton 2004):

- Firstly, an initial lack of trust and understanding among the sectors proved to be a major barrier to successful partnerships. During the wargame the teams realized that they did not address the broader group of stakeholders but focused instead on their own employees and customers. All participants realized that the failure to address the needs of high-risk and marginalized communities, such as commercial sex workers, intravenous drug users, and the mobile population, reduced the effectiveness of their response.

- Secondly, the social and cultural stigma associated with HIV/AIDS proved detrimental to prevention, testing, and treatment. The social and cultural mores of India prevented the open discussion of many high-risk behaviors, making it difficult to educate the population about even the most basic methods of prevention.

- Thirdly, voluntary counseling and testing services were underutilized because of a lack of available care and treatment. People were reluctant to undergo testing not only because of the stigma but because testing was not supported by adequate care and support services for those found to be HIV positive.

- Fourthly, the healthcare infrastructure, both in terms of facilities and human resources, was not sufficiently large to deal with the potential size of the epidemic. During the wargame the teams discovered that the existing infrastructure and HIV/AIDS education and training were inadequate to support interventions.

- Fifthly, long-term provision of treatment transforms HIV from a fatal disease to a chronic illness with increasing demands on healthcare infrastructure and available resources.

During the wargame the success of the teams in developing effective interventions led to a new set of issues and challenges itself. AIDS-related prejudice was reduced, but overall prevalence and healthcare cost were predicted to increase, because of the longer life expectancies of those infected with HIV/AIDS. Others feared that an increase in antiretroviral therapy could lead to complacency towards prevention, increasing the number of individuals in need for treatment over time.

LESSONS LEARNED

As the teams responded to the variety of challenges during the wargame, four critical success factors became evident (Booz Allen Hamilton 2004):

- Leadership from the top is vital, whether it be from government officials, CEOs, or community leaders. This should emphasize that a strong public stance on HIV/AIDS lays the groundwork for broad participation across all sectors, addressing key barriers such as stigma and discrimination.

- Non-discrimination, awareness and prevention, voluntary counseling and testing, care, support, and treatment all rely on each other. The wargame also illustrated that targeted early actions are often the least expensive interventions, and that they can prevent the longer-term cost of delivering treatment. In addition, proactive action targeting high-risk groups can prevent the disease from spreading to the general population.

- Collaborative partnerships, for example, between the business sector and NGOs, are essential in order to maximize impact.

- Clear prioritization of programs and innovative funding approaches are critical given resource and infrastructure constraints. The teams noted the need for a coordinated approach to funding at a national level, making sure that the program supports the national strategy and objectives, but also emphasized the need for decentralized funding to deliver funds as quickly as possible to those who are in need. During the wargame itself a number of innovative approaches to funding were articulated.

Having simulated ten years over the course of two days, the participants needed to come up with team actions to help mitigate the future growth of the epidemic and its impact on the nation's health and economy. HIV/AIDS prevalence, incidence, and mortality compared to the base scenario (doing nothing) might be reduced by more than 50 percent. Additionally, the impact of HIV/AIDS on the economy was minimized and GDP loss was reduced by an astonishing $31.5 billion, and the loss in discretionary spending was reduced by $9.2 billion.

The teams initiated and explored a total of 53 partnerships, proposed 100 new initiatives ranging from business initiatives to raise awareness and increase access to testing and treatment, to government prevention efforts at a national level. The wargame clearly underlined the need for moving forward in greater collaboration between the public and private sector. Nations needed to evaluate the risks accurately and set funding priorities. Overall government funding and resource mobilization to fight HIV/AIDS needed to be dramatically increased. Donor countries should be encouraged to contribute more through bilateral and international initiatives.

In addition, developing countries should be pushed to prioritize health issues on the national agenda. National governments needed to maximize platforms for business sector involvement in response to the epidemic, and ensure direct and sustained participation by business leaders on National HIV/AIDS Committees and the Global Fund Coordinating Mechanisms.

Business sector skills could be applied to government strategies to improve the reach and effectiveness of HIV/AIDS programs. Investment partnerships between the public and private sectors would also help to scale up existing initiatives. For example, existing corporate infrastructure and skills can be used in the broader community and in order to seek support from international donors for community programs. Finally, business, government, and community executives needed to ensure strong leadership and advocacy. Public acknowledgement of the epidemic, and the need for urgent action to address the stigma and discrimination that had allowed the epidemic to spread unchecked for the past 20 years, would inspire others to take action.

Case Study: Bioterrorism[2]

POINT OF DEPARTURE

After the 9/11 terrorist attacks, the US quickly realized that terrorism was no longer a problem primarily surfacing outside of the country, but that it could strike deep within its own borders and with an order of magnitude that was previously unthinkable. All of a sudden planners at the Pentagon and in Langley were no longer restricted in their thinking, and scenarios, previously considered too far-fetched, were afforded great scrutiny.

In the weeks that followed 9/11 a second threat filled the news: anthrax. Letters with suspicious white powder surfaced in multiple locations and the threat of a bioterrorism attack within the US became suddenly very real. Partly as a result of these developments, the US government decided to run a

---

2   Information taken from Ahlquist and Burns (2002).

simulation to anticipate the full effect a bioterrorism attack could have on the country. They sought to see how well America was prepared in response to such a scenario.

OBJECTIVE AND QUESTIONS

One objective of this wargame was to involve top leaders from medical products companies, healthcare providers, insurers and government agencies and have them jointly deal with a hypothetical, but absolutely realistic, bioterrorism attack on the US. The aim was to confront the participants with the realities, dilemmas and consequences of alternative actions and to test how well the cooperation between the constituents would work.

What would be discovered during the wargame should help lay the foundation for improvements to structures, processes, and general preparation should a similar event ever take place. The purpose of the wargame was not to predict the future, but rather to raise the level of awareness amongst all the participants of what could happen, what would work and what would not work, so that all could better prepare for the future.

GAME SETUP

The wargame was sponsored, structured and prepared by Booz Allen Hamilton and The Council for Excellence in Government. The latter organization was founded in 1983 by a small group of business leaders who had served in government and wished to create a strong independent voice for excellence in government. The aim of the council is to improve the performance of government and the connections between government and citizens.

In total 75 government and healthcare professionals participated in the wargame, bringing together senior policy makers in the Department of Health and Human Services, the Federal Emergency Management Agency, the Department of Defense, the Department of Veteran Affairs, state and local government, business participants—including CEOs and other senior executives from medical products companies, including pharma and biotech— and healthcare providers, such as hospitals, health maintenance organization s (HMOs), physicians, insurers, and health industry associations.

To enable participants to cope with the multiple stakeholders, they were organized into three business stakeholder teams, three government stakeholder teams and a control team (see Figure 5.2).

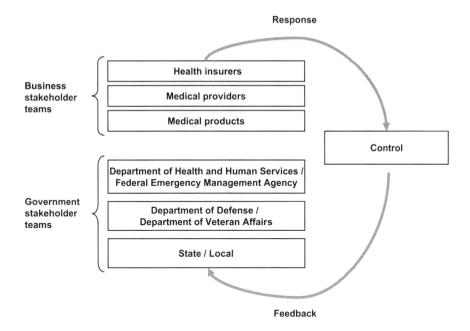

Figure 5.2   Team structure overview

The wargame opened with the following scenario: pneumonic plague bacteria in aerosol form were released simultaneously in two major cities in a coordinated terrorist attack. Although initial symptoms resemble the common flu, the pneumonic plague is nearly 100 percent fatal if not treated early with powerful antibiotics, and, unlike anthrax or West Nile Disease, it is highly contagious. The simulated epidemic was unleashed in Detroit (Michigan), and Norfolk (Virginia).

Simulated on the basis of real-world epidemiological models, the spread of the disease from its points of origination could be modeled quite accurately. As in the HIV/AIDS simulation the spread could be affected by a variety of factors, such as vaccination programs, quarantine measures, restriction of travel and so on.

Over the course of the game the participants identified a number of challenges, which would make it difficult to respond effectively to a bioterrorism attack:

- In the first place, biological warfare agents, unlike natural disasters or peacetime epidemics, spread rapidly; this is further accelerated by releasing the agent simultaneously in multiple locations.

- Secondly, the rapid overload of the local healthcare system and widespread panic stresses law enforcement and other social services to the breaking point.

- Thirdly, whilst the immediate responders are all local, decision making on issues such as where and how to allocate available antibiotics; how to inform and educate the public; and when and where to close borders and restrict traffic, must move quickly to the national level once the magnitude of the problem becomes evident.

Traditionally, neither private industry nor many government agencies have played active roles in homeland security, which has been almost exclusively the domain of the Department of Defense. The result was that the interaction between these players often proved difficult due to the unclear distribution of competencies and ambiguous chains of command.

The extreme contagiousness of the pneumonic plague, and the lack of a vaccine, called for both quarantine and the rapid and extensive prophylactic treatment of uninfected individuals with antibiotics: this proved a significant challenge to the teams during the wargame—especially since the quarantining of large parts of the population raised civil liberties and law enforcement issues and offered no easy answers. The need for widespread prophylaxis would strain drug supplies and leave the country vulnerable to new attacks or naturally occurring epidemics. Logistic issues, such as how to deliver vaccines and drugs to millions of people, raised insurmountable obstacles. In sum the following key challenges were raised (Ahlquist and Burns 2002):

1. To react quickly, industry needed a single point of contact with the government, but at the time, multiple contact points existed.

2. Aggressive containment and prophylaxis can limit the spread of the disease, but moving too quickly may consume reserve capacity needed for future threats elsewhere.

3. Response plans normally focus efforts at the local level, but bioterrorism quickly becomes a national problem.

4. Suspending legal, regulatory, and procedural constraints may be necessary to meet immediate needs, but such steps can create serious downstream consequences for public health and business viability.

Subsequently the teams discovered that the difference between a controlled outbreak and a massive epidemic ultimately hinged on a few critical success factors (Ahlquist and Burns 2002, 3):

- "Leadership: confusion about 'who's in charge' in just the first days of the attack had major consequences during the weeks that followed.

- Knowledge: participants agreed that thousands of lives depended on ready information about pharmaceutical and medical equipment stockpiles throughout the nation.

- Coordination: individual companies and local governments responded well, but what mattered most was immediate and quick coordination between companies, across agencies and among states."

LESSONS LEARNED

A major lesson was that at the time the levels of preparation and response in place in the US were not adequate, but that the existing levels of preparation could be improved. The US might cope with a bioterrorism attack, but only if the response were rapid, coordinated across business and government, well prepared, and thought out ahead of time.

The teams further discovered that massive, immediate action was required, but they also found that the lack of a common language between government and industry, and then a lack of a single point of contact between these groups stymied the rapid movement needed. No mechanisms were in place to enable quick coordination across agencies and businesses to mobilize the resources available. The teams concluded that the government alone couldn't protect the American people from bioterrorism, hence the need to mobilize business resources.

Prior planning and practice proved the key to enable rapid response, which would be critical in limiting the damage. Mechanisms were needed to collect and share information on pharmaceutical and equipment stockpiles before and during crises. Preparedness would require new levels of communication and cooperation across public/private, local/national, and military/civilian boundaries. Further, building and sharing knowledge would mean assessing potential actions and their impact. Epidemiological models needed to be developed for the most common hazardous bioagents, exploring the impact of actions such as quarantine and prophylaxis. Above all, the information needed to be shared across government and industry. This sharing required new policies, protocols, and mechanisms to coordinate government and business response. Response policies needed to be integrated across federal, state, and local government, and among healthcare businesses in order to clarify roles and responsibilities, and to identify the key point of contact and authority.

The wargame enabled the teams to conclude, that private/public partnerships can improve bioterrorism preparation and response by identifying and involving relevant participants; establishing agreed roles and responsibilities; sharing information on stockpiles and surge capacity; pre-defining economic, legal, and liability parameters and limits; and coordinating public awareness and education. In addition, the wargame was able to give the mixed groups of participants a rapid education in how other organizations think and act, as well as providing a first check on ideas and suggestions, highlighting the need for a new kind of public/private partnership in homeland security in the US.

Developing Foresight   CHAPTER

6

While developing foresight is widely perceived as a crucial activity for any organization, in particular in an increasingly dynamic and complex business environment, the question of how to develop foresight remains difficult to answer. This chapter offers a contribution to answering that question.

Having emphasized the importance of developing foresight, the case studies in the chapter underline how business wargames can help corporations in the process. The first case study will demonstrate how wargaming has been used in an attempt to develop foresight for an entire industry, in this case asset management, and then we will discuss briefly the application of business wargaming to assess future power shifts in the public sector during the cold war.

Developing Foresight in Business Wargaming

Alfred North Whitehead identified "foresight" in a celebrated lecture at the Harvard Business School in 1931, as the crucial feature of the competent business mind (Tsoukas 2004). In the recent past others have encouraged corporations with increasing urgency to develop foresight (e.g. Hamel and Prahalad 1994; Courtney 2001).

Makridakis (2004, XIII) defines foresight as follows: "The role of foresight is to provide business executives and government policy makers with ways of seeing the future with different eyes and fully understanding the possible implications of alternative technological/societal paths." Foresight is more about spotting developments before they become trends, seeing patterns before they fully emerge, and grasping the relevant features of social currents that are likely to have an impact (Tsoukas 2004), than it is about making predictions. In short, developing foresight is about recognizing weak signals of change in the corporate business environment and it is about imagining alternative scenarios and how one's own organization is likely to evolve within them. Day and Schoemaker (2006, 1–2) articulate the relevance of spotting weak signals as follows: "The key is to quickly spot those signals that are relevant and explore them further, filter out the noise, and pursue opportunities ahead of the competition or recognize the early signs of trouble before they escalate into major problems."

Hamel and Prahalad (1995) are convinced that an organization which does not develop a picture of the future, which does not develop foresight, is most likely not involved in the future. They emphasize that the success of a company depends on its ability to reach the future before its competitors. Courtney (2001) emphasizes the importance of dealing differently with uncertainties, by improving the foresight capabilities of organizations, especially in planning processes. Bazerman and Watkins (2004) argue that organizations are facing two groups of surprises: predictable surprises and unpredictable surprises. Predictable surprises can be recognized on the horizon, but arise when managers fail to spot them or fail to respond to them. However, it is essential to develop foresight in the first place in order even to recognize predictable surprises, or weak signals of change.

Business wargaming can be perceived as a tool to develop foresight, recognize predictable surprises, and spot weak signals of change, especially when a business wargame is designed to project several years into the future, so that the participants are forced to think ahead, to review their assumptions about tomorrow critically, and to question their mental models. We believe that the great advantage of business wargaming is, that it is not only analytical but also most importantly participative. Bazerman and Watkins (2004), for instance, argue that cognitive flaws have been identified as the key reasons why change or strategic surprises have not been identified in time by organizations. These cognitive flaws or defense mechanisms are more likely to be recognized by applying a tool, which is participative, allowing managers to actually experience future events, making the case for business wargaming.

The Future of Asset Management Distribution[1]

POINT OF DEPARTURE

The second Thought Leadership Summit (TLS) held in 2006 in Monaco was devoted to applying business wargaming as a means to explore the future distribution of asset management. The game was designed and executed by Yale Professor Paul Bracken.

---

1   Information taken from The Thought Leadership Summit (2006).

The asset management industry is characterized by enormous complexity; there are thousands of suppliers managing 46,000 funds, and as many as 4,000 distributors, which are often complex organizations with very complex needs. In addition, organizations operating in this industry are confronted with an ever-changing environment, including, for example, changes in stock markets, customer needs, and regulations.

In the context of this wargame the term "distribution" refers to the distribution of funds:

> *So depending on what perspective you choose, a fund can be distributed twice, first from the "manufacturers" (i.e. asset managers) to the distributor, and then from the distributor to its end client. Distribution here means the process by which "manufacturers" form and maintain relationships with their intermediates ..." (Thought Leadership Summit 2006, 41)*

OBJECTIVES AND QUESTIONS

A study by PricewaterhouseCoopers conducted in 2006 revealed that distribution was the most vital area of strategic focus for asset management firms. The main objective of the wargame was to focus on this issue; to develop alternative views of the future of asset management distribution in Europe and what implications these views might have for strategic decision making in the present. The following are the goals as stated (Thought Leadership Summit 2006, 18) for the business wargame:

- "To exercise and simulate the future of distribution under the conditions of the given e-Volution scenario

- To learn about different strategies and market behaviours of different players

- To develop and test a distribution navigator for the industry ..."

GAME SETUP

Prior to the execution of the actual game in Monaco, 40 industry strategists from 30 firms were interviewed and asked to share the key European distribution challenges for the asset management industry, as they saw them; in total, 21 key issues were defined. These served as a "discussion starter" at the beginning of the preparation phase for the business wargame.

A scenario was formulated to establish the conditions of the business wargame. The scenario, called "e-Volution", described a world in which the promises of technology were met in the context of the next generation of the internet and convergence in technologies and media. In this context the industry evolves to support two groups; large players dominating global distribution and very small ones, which are highly specialized. The clients have greater access to information and to effective analytical tools. They demand value, clarity in pricing, reporting and performance. In addition, progress has been made in harmonizing and standardizing the industry regulations across the region.

In contrast to some of the other cases we have described in this book, this particular business wargame was built around two moves; the first simulated a time period from 2006 to 2009 and the second move a period up to 2013. The teams presented their strategies at the end of each round, which were than evaluated after each move. The participants were asked to structure their work, according to a strategy worksheet, around the following topics: client–value proposition, product strategy, distribution revenue model, and possible mergers, acquisitions and divestitures. They were also supplied with player profiles, giving them detailed information on the stakeholders they were representing for the purpose of the game.

During the moves the teams were allowed to communicate with each other about acquisitions, alliances, and oversight via email. Interestingly, however, participants were shifted between the teams, in order to simulate a market characterized by merger, alliances, spinouts and new ventures.

The previously mentioned distribution navigator was developed prior to the business wargame with the aim of measuring the way the various stakeholders in the wargame changed over time. Summarizing the 21 identified core issues into four axes led to the development of the "distribution navigator." Each of these axes described a core industry issue (Thought Leadership Summit 2006, 92):

- "The macro and geographical context: is the industry a single European market, or is it a collection of country markets?

- What is being sold: are offerings merely products, or are they in fact solutions to client needs?

- Balance of power between manufacturers and distributors: does power lie with manufacturers or distributors?

- How are offerings being sold: are they bought or are they required to be sold?"

The wargame was concluded with a plenary discussion and an analysis on the findings from the two moves. Thirty-seven asset managers were invited to participate in the wargame, as well as eight observers from leading industry companies. The participants were assigned to one of six teams, each representing an industry stakeholder. The following stakeholders were represented:

- large universal bank e.g. Deutsche Bank

- asset management firm e.g. Threadneedle Investments

- national regulator e.g. AMF (Autorité des Marchés Financières)

- network of advisers e.g. MLP AG

- insurance e.g. Allianz Global Investors

- e-Platform e.g. Cortal Consors.

LESSONS LEARNED

Following the game, the various lessons learned were summarized as per a mind map. Concern was raised under the heading "diffusion and confusion" that the industry faced a dilemma: on the one hand, it was extremely profitable and on the other hand there was confusion about how the industry would develop in the future and what the strategies should be to meet the future challenges.

A second lesson that emerged was the need for a discussion on the overall framework for the industry. It appeared in the business wargame that the asset management industry is an introverted economy that needs to open itself towards ideas and strategies from the outside. The wargaming also revealed the dilemma for the larger players in the industry in positioning themselves either as manufacturer or as a distributor. By contrast, the smaller players showed greater flexibility, even though their actions were dependent on the strategic behavior of the larger players.

The regulator, who plays a very important role in this particular industry, was seen during the first move as a limiting and purely technical constraint, likely to hinder innovation. However, this perception changed during the second move. Not only did participants state that they could now understand why regulation is so time consuming, but they also increased their communication with the regulators in the second move. This left some of the participants with the distinct lesson that regulators too can contribute to the process of innovation. These results reinforced the perception that the asset management industry is very introverted. The business wargame underlined the importance of getting in touch with the client, and relating more to the end customer. As a whole the wargame allowed its participants a relatively detailed look at the future of the distribution of asset management and certainly helped them develop a forward view of the industry.

THE CASE OF ALLIANZ GLOBAL INVESTORS

To be a little more specific, we will now look in more detail at one of the players represented in the business wargame: Allianz Global Investors.

The team representing Allianz saw its core value proposition in preparing Germans for the future. In the simulated period up to 2009, the Allianz team aimed at building its investment capabilities with an internal asset management factory and also by complementing it with external products. Concerning its M&A (mergers and acquisitions) activities, the team tried to buy 50 percent of Threadneedle and to exchange its Dresdner Bank for DWS, the asset management company of Deutsche Bank; it also opened negotiations with Cortal.

While all of these deals were rejected in the end, by 2013 Allianz had focused more clearly on its role as a packager and distributor, forming links with companies such as the just mentioned DWS and with the, also explicitly played, financial service supplier MLP. Overall, the lesson learned for the Allianz team was that the team believed that it was a mistake to try to build investment performance in house.

Wargames in the Public Sector

Wargaming in the public sector has a long tradition in the US. During the Cold War in particular the US government was looking for insight into how various scenarios and developments would play out and what the consequences for its foreign policy might be. Between 1987 and 1989 a series of wargames was carried out, focusing on the change in global power structures over the next 40 years. The objective of these wargames was to determine how global power would change, particularly in terms of the future roles of the European Community, Japan, the US, the USSR, the Middle East, and the People's Republic of China. While these games remain poorly publicized and little is known about the specific findings and the consequences for national policy, at a strategic level, these wargames suggested the following likely developments:

- The USSR would fail economically and fall apart.

- Japan would be unable to become a global superpower.

- Eastern Europe would open to the West without intervention by the USSR.

- East and West Germany will quickly unite without intervention by the USSR.

Whilst today these findings may all seem obvious, at the time of the first of these games, people could not believe what they were experiencing. In fact, they doubted the predictive power of the simulation and played the game repeatedly with different participants. Despite this the same basic findings emerged with each game—the rest is history.

What is interesting is that at the time, the People's Republic of China was not playing a major role. India too was never perceived as the economic power that it has turned out to be over the same period of time. Were the game to be played again today, the scenario would unfold somewhat differently with these two countries, Russia and Brazil playing increasingly important roles in the world's economy as the source of much of the global manufacturing, services, fuel and agricultural production.

Another game in the late 1980s, the results of which remain largely classified, revolved around the Strategic Defense Initiative (SDI). The initial idea of the program was to establish a leak-proof missile defense shield over the territory of the United States in order to prevent any effective nuclear attack. The question underlying this game was: how much strategic defense is absolutely required given the deterrence effect, and what would be the resources needed to achieve it?

The wargame produced some extraordinary insight, because contrary to conventional wisdom at the time—which suggested that a complete and leak-proof shield was needed—the wargame actually suggested that a shield, effectively covering only 10 percent of the territory would have nearly the same deterrent effect as a complete shield, as long as the 10 percent shield could be deployed in a mobile form which kept any enemy guessing as to its exact position.

This was based on the insight that if the Union of Soviet Socialist Republics (USSR) wanted to ensure a similar first-strike hit rate, it would need to fire as many rockets to counter the defensive effect of a 10 percent shield as it would to counter a complete shield, making any attack extremely costly. At the same time the deterrent effect from the perspective of the US could be achieved with far fewer resources than initially anticipated. These findings led to a complete change in US policy with respect to the program under the conditions of the Cold War.

Change Management

Business wargaming can be considered a very powerful change management tool as well. As previously explained, every wargame functions as a change management tool on one level or other, simply because it brings a group of people together and has them work jointly on a common challenge. The insights they gain and the increased understanding of the other participants involved initiate a process of change. However, there are some wargames that turn out to be catalysts of change that extend far beyond just the top management team. In our view, wargaming as a tool for the savvy change manager will gain more recognition in the years to come. If applied in the right context it is an extremely effective way of driving change.

Change Management and Business Wargaming

Change is the only constant in today's corporate world. While this aphorism seems to have a universal application, it appears that the pace of change nowadays is increasing. The continuous change within business environments requires organizations to reinvent themselves on a regular basis, in order to adapt. Any process of change within an organization will face resistance. The roots of this resistance can be found in fear and a survival instinct which operate at several levels to protect social systems from painful experiences of loss, distress, chaos, and the emotions associated with change (Jarrett 2003). However, Duck (2001) makes the argument that change unfolds in a reasonably predictable and manageable series of phases.

Introducing a business wargame prior to a change program has the great benefit of enabling you to test how the change process may evolve and, in particular, which obstacles to change may emerge. Forewarning of this kind enables you to anticipate and counter obstacles before they occur. In the context of change management within the military, wargames have been applied in the transformation of the armed forces (Starr 2001).

By allowing the participants of a business wargame to view a situation with the benefit of a different perspective, it is possible to highlight the requirement (case for change) to change a strategy or an organization and to enable the participants to experience the likely effect of that change, before it happens.

Case Study: Changing the Game[1]

In the early 1990s, a large plastics company was confronted by new and aggressive competitors entering the market, which it previously *owned*. Not only did these new competitors enter the market, but they also pursued the company's top customers very single-mindedly and managed to take a significant chunk of the business away from the company. Slightly bemused at what was going on, the CEO took the decision to commission a business wargame to explore what was happening and what the company might do to stop this loss of market share.

During the simulation it became clear that they were losing business largely due to their entrenched way of thinking about the business and a cultural inertia that prevented them from doing something about it. What the game revealed was that the way the products in the business were sold had fundamentally changed. The company had learned to use price as the main driver to close the sale but competitors were pushing other buttons with customers, selling them added-value features such as consistency, quality and so on.

Think of it this way: global corporations, such as McDonald's, do value the fact that the yellow of their arches remains the same on all their premises, be it in the US, Paris, London, Budapest, Bangkok, Shanghai, or Singapore. If they get this kind of consistency from a supplier, who has to buy the raw materials in order to provide that consistency, they are willing to pay for it as it constitutes an important element of their global brand and price is far less important than consistency of quality.

In the face of this unwelcome new situation, the company realized that their corporate culture was not in tune with the changes occurring in their market. Sales and marketing departments, in particular, were forced to respond to this new situation and adapt to the new rules, which were changing business the way they knew it. On the back of the insights gleaned from the original game, the company commissioned consultants to train a team of their own

---

1   Information taken from a public speech by George E. Thibault, then Principal with Booz Allen Hamilton, at the Swiss General Staff College, 2001.

people to be able to run the game repeatedly with the sales forces in their own organization.

Following the training the group of internal coaches embarked on a trip to enable all the largest sales and marketing departments to experience the game and find out for themselves what they needed to do. By looking through the eyes of their competitors and customers, the sales teams quickly realized what needed to be done and went about implementing the necessary changes. The first-hand lessons learned from the wargame significantly accelerated the change process in the sales and marketing departments and allowed the organization to defend market share effectively and regain customers who had been lost to the competition. Having seen the effects of the game on his sales numbers, the CEO correctly summarized: "One sale—previously lost—actually paid for the entire simulation!"

Education and Recruitment

CHAPTER

8

Yet another effective application of business wargaming is in the area of education and recruitment. This chapter explores the application of the wargaming methodology for management education in a business context. In addition, we will show how wargaming has been successfully applied in a recruiting context for consulting firm Booz Allen Hamilton in its successful "CEO Challenge" program.

Business Wargaming in Education and Recruiting

As outlined in Chapter One, business education was the first application of wargaming methodology in a corporate context in business games or management games. Faria and Dickinson (1994) point out several benefits of applying a business wargame in management education:

- *Orient and train new employees*: a wargame can give a newly hired employee the opportunity to gain decision-making experience in the new company.

- *Screen current managers or would-be managers*: during the course of a business wargame, for instance, analytical or decision-making skills can be assessed.

- *Ongoing management training*: applying business wargaming in management development has several advantages. They allow executives to work on their decision skills, experiment with strategies, learn new analytical tools, identify areas of further training, and gain various insights in, for instance, their own organizations, competitors, and in general other stakeholders.

Practical Applications

We now offer two examples of the application of business wargaming for training and development in an organizational context and for educational purposes in business schools.

TRAINING AND DEVELOPMENT

One potential application for business wargaming in an organizational context is to familiarize newly hired employees with the organization, in particular with its capabilities. This is especially powerful in organizations involved in project work and similar situations where people with different skill sets need to work together successfully. Such settings may include consulting firms, investment banks, private equity boutiques, executive search firms, IT service companies and the like.

At the start of this form of business wargame, for instance, capability cards are handed out to the participants, representing the knowledge, skills and background of individuals throughout the firm. Based on this information, the participants are required to make sense of all this know-how in order to pitch to a market team for the right to manage a series of projects. The objectives of the game are the following:

- Leverage the full capabilities of an organization by learning about capabilities within other teams.

- Increase collaboration by learning about the capabilities of others in the organization.

- Gain new insights into building a business (i.e. synthesize existing knowledge and package it for new pitches).

- Emphasize competitive bidding strategies.

- Most important of all, meet and learn about other employees in the same organization.

Such a business wargame has the benefit of allowing newly hired employees as well as existing members of the organization to think more strategically about their business and not just focus on short-term revenue generation. It also allows employees to experience and think at different levels of the organization, thus again fostering a shared level of knowledge and capability throughout the organization.

"THE BATTLE FOR THE CLICKS"[1]

Business wargames have also been applied in education contexts, for instance, by the consultancy Fuld & Company. In April 2005 they organized a business wargame between MBA students from the Harvard Business School and MIT's Sloan School of Management (Fuld 2006).

This business wargame, called *The Battle for Clicks*, evolved around internet advertising, with Harvard students representing Microsoft and Time Warner, and the MIT students playing the roles of Yahoo! and Google. The wargame was conducted over a single day and evolved over eight hours. The teams faced the following issues (Fuld 2006, 80–1):

- "Can Google (whose stock price has soared to $300 a share) continue to defy the laws of competitive gravity?

- Google depends currently on its search engine advertising model. It's a one-note company with 95 percent of the company's sales coming from this one revenue source. How can it diversify or build on this base before its market share erodes from new entrants in the internet search business?

- How can AOL, Time Warner's division, slow down the rapid loss of subscribers? Can it find a way to leverage Time Warner's valuable content, in the form of its rich family of magazines, broadcast group, and cable network?

- What can Microsoft do to prevent or at least slow down Google's hijacking of the desktop through such ingenious tools as Google Desktop? Will Microsoft's MNM search engine be powerful enough to grab share of the click for advertising away from Google?

- How can Yahoo! break out of the pack? Despite its expanded search capabilities and revenue that equal that of Google, it can very easily lose its focus as it moves in many directions at once."

Alongside a lead facilitator to overlook this business wargame, four judges were appointed each with a relevant background to this game, with the goal of adding expertise and insight to the wargame. However, the task of the judges was also to review and evaluate each of the teams, based on criteria such as "insight into their strategic positioning, accuracy in presenting the

---

1   Information taken from Fuld (2006).

facts, creativity in proposing a new strategy, and foresight into the near future" (Fuld, 2006: 99).

According to Fuld (2006), the most difficult task for the students at the beginning of the simulation was to make the transition from being a student to acting as a manager for the company they were assigned to. In order to add to the dynamic nature of the business wargame, a surprise external economic event was introduced: a rise in communication taxes, along with the suggestion that state taxation of the internet, could possibly hinder growth in internet advertising.

The benefit for the students, besides being introduced to the business wargaming methodology, was that they had the opportunity to apply their knowledge of their business environment, in a dynamic strategic simulation. This involved them in a level of discussion that in real life would have taken place at a very much more senior level in the organization. and it enabled them to experience how their strategic decision making would perform in a dynamic environment.

Applying Business Wargaming in a University Context[2]

We have already briefly touched on the potential applications of business wargaming in universities. In this case study we will describe in more detail how business wargaming can be applied to the education of students at a masters level in strategy.

POINT OF DEPARTURE

This particular business wargame was carried out at a German university. It was intended to give masters-level students in management and cultural studies an opportunity to add to their knowledge on strategy and strategic management gained during previous semesters.

OBJECTIVES AND QUESTIONS

Clearly, the main objectives for the students were to apply their theoretical knowledge on strategy and strategy formulation in a simulation. In addition, because of the particular setup of this wargame, another objective was introduced: to enable the students to experience the relevance of competitive intelligence (in particular competitive analysis) in strategy. One last objective

---

2   Jan Oliver Schwarz applies business wargaming on a regular basis for teaching management
     students.

was to introduce students to tools for developing competitive intelligence such as business wargaming and strategic early warning systems.

GAME SETUP

In this wargame the German music industry was simulated over three moves covering a period from 2007 till 2015. Around 25 students took part in the wargame, organized into five teams (see Figure 8.1).

The facilitators of the seminar and of the business wargame took on the role of the control team. Several weeks prior to the business wargame the students were assigned to their stakeholders. Once the students had been assigned to their group, they were asked to prepare the player profile for the stakeholder they were representing in the simulation. All the students received a template in which they were asked to prepare ten slides for their player, containing general information on their player, the industry, their relevant market, also including a SWOT (strengths, weaknesses, opportunities, threats) and PEST (political, economical, social, technological) analysis. The market and customer group, for instance, was asked to come up with an idea how the market was segmented and what the needs of these segments were. Unlike the other business wargames we have described so far, in this instance the participants of the wargame were actually responsible for assembling the gamebook.

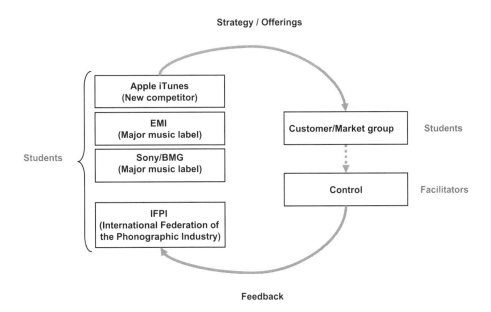

Figure 8.1   Team structure overview

The game was carried out over two and half days, and opened with an introduction to business wargaming by the facilitators. Following this the students presented the information they had gathered on their particular player to one another. The wargame actually started on the morning of the next day and ended around early afternoon of the third day. All the pre-prepared information was distributed to each team.

While the stakeholder teams were preparing their presentation, the market and customer team were asked to come up with ideas on how to evaluate the moves and how to give feedback. In particular, using a quantitative model would not be satisfying, since the IFPI (International Federation of the Phonographic Industry) was involved in the wargame as a player and is not a competitor in the music industry. So the students developed criteria from the perspective of the market and customers for the basis on which to evaluate the strategies of each team and on which to provide feedback to them.

During the simulation, time slots were issued by the control team, which allowed the students to communicate amongst one another via email in order to strike deals or form alliances. The control team assumed the role of stakeholders not represented in the business wargame. They also introduced a number of external stimuli during the moves, such as a press release, which added to the complexity and the dynamics of the simulation. The wargame ended with a lengthy discussion reflecting not only on the weekend, but in particular on what the students had learned during the simulation and how this related to their knowledge from their previous lectures on strategy and strategic management.

LESSONS LEARNED

At this point rather than analyzing the single moves in this wargame or the strategies formulated in the context of the German music industry, we will focus on the overall lessons from the perspective of business strategy.

The first important lesson for the students was the particular relevance of good and solid competitive intelligence. Of course, the information gathered and then presented by the students on their assigned stakeholder, varied in quality, in some cases, significantly. Indeed, those teams with only mediocre competitive intelligence struggled during the first move to come up with a convincing strategy.

During the preparation phases those teams with the least convincing stakeholder profiles were mainly concerned with figuring out who the competitors and customers were and what differentiated their own player from the others. It appeared that some teams were never able to overcome this early disadvantage during the entire business wargame. This left those students with an insight how important rigorous and solid competitive analysis and intelligence are for formulating a strategy and competing in a market.

Overall, the students experienced that formulating a strategy is a highly complex and difficult task, particularly when juggling the different variables that are of relevance. Therefore it was not too surprising, that in the first move the students focused well on the customers in their strategies but neglected the fact that they had competitors. On the other hand, some teams had difficulty in anticipating changes in customer behavior over the time, while others focused too heavily on technological developments. The students also experienced difficulty in coming up with a strategy in a given time, especially when presented with information overload and an overabundance of choice, with inadequate time to discuss their decisions.

This business wargame provided the students with very valuable insights on formulating strategy and what it takes for a good competitive analysis. In addition, the simulation highlighted not only the relevance of business wargaming as a means of testing strategy, but also the relevance of competitive intelligence in general and of tools such as strategic early warning systems to help organization, to detect early signals of the need for change.

"This was the best seminar I went to during my time at university," one student stated when asked to give feedback on this form of seminar. Overall, the feedback from the students was overwhelmingly positive, emphasizing how much they enjoyed this form of "action learning." Considering this feedback and the dynamics during the simulation, the value of business wargaming as a means for teaching strategy even outside of university campuses is convincing and, as we see in the next case study, some companies have even made it a case in point to provide this learning experience to students

Case Study: The Booz Allen CEO Challenge[3]

The Booz Allen CEO Challenge in its current form was launched by one of the authors and his team in 2005 at Harvard Business School and the Kellogg School of Management. It has since been played at many top business schools in the US and in Europe and already has been recognized as a tool for creating

---

3   Public information, www.ceo-challenge.com, and personal insights of the authors.

an employer brand (Rodriguez 2006). The current case study used for the CEO challenge simulates the development of the portable audio device industry in the US.

POINT OF DEPARTURE

Although Booz Allen Hamilton is one of the top players in the strategy consulting field, it has never been recognized for it and has thus never been a household name like some of its main competitors, like, for example, McKinsey & Company, The Boston Consulting Group or Bain & Company. There are multiple reasons for this. For one, the company has never pursued a strategy that would give it that household name status and remains rather conservative in its communication with the greater public. The company is also actually still comprised of two businesses: the strategy consulting division and a division which is more government/technology oriented. This can often lead to a misconception about what the company is really all about and how it is positioned on campus.

Following the downturn after the dot-com bust, the company lost some of its standing at top business schools because it simply stopped recruiting from them and consequently did not sustain a high enough presence. As the economy recovered and business picked up again, the firm found itself at a disadvantage when competing for top talents from the best business schools in the world because not enough people knew the company and even fewer knew that it was involved in actual strategy work. When looking for an effective way to change this perception, a group of people involved in the recruiting activities of the company decided to leverage the firm's wargaming expertise and devise a scaled-down game that could be played with business students without lengthy preparation or the need for particular industry expertise. Therefore cases were chosen, which had a clear consumer orientation and involved products/services with which the students could familiarize themselves quickly.

OBJECTIVE

The objective was to create a high-intensity event that would be attended by some of the brightest minds to be found at the top MBA programs and show them first hand what it feels like to sit on the executive board of a large company or act as a consultant to such a company. The students needed to work hard, think in a structured and strategic way and come up with specific action plans to establish how they wanted to win! Aside from the actual simulation they should be given ample opportunity to mix with Booz Allen Hamilton representatives and learn about consulting and the company. The event also provided a great opportunity for the Booz Allen people to observe the students in a high-pressure, high-performance environment and assess their behavior in a team setting.

Besides promoting the firm, its people and the high-level work it does, the CEO Challenge serves as an important relationship management tool from which 30 students graduate at each event. Moreover, those students who do not make it through the rigorous selection process act as valuable ambassadors for the firm when they return to their schools and help raise awareness about the quality of work and the people at Booz Allen. In promoting the event to prospective participants, the firm used tag lines such as:

> *Do you have what it takes to excel in the top job?*

> *You're the head of a major electronics company playing in the portable music device market. One of your biggest competitors is poised to roll out an incredible new device, implementing the latest technology and the coolest design features — six months ahead of schedule.*

> *What do you do?*

> *Test your corner-office savvy in a fast-paced, high-stakes strategy simulation that puts you head-to-head with your peers. The CEO Challenge is a chance to demonstrate strategic thinking and teamwork and to prove your worth – with the pros watching your every move!*

The event puts students in the shoes of a CEO and clearly challenges them, hence the name "CEO Challenge."

GAME SETUP

The CEO Challenge is a two and a half day event, typically played over a weekend. It includes 30 hand-selected students from top MBA schools and approximately five to eight consultants, who moderate and coach the students as well as take care of logistics and IT. The event starts with a detailed introduction to strategy and strategic planning and what role wargaming plays, followed by a basic anatomy of wargaming and a presentation of relevant case studies, some of which are outlined in this book. The presentations then get more specific, involving a crash course in the audio device market (the industry setting of the CEO Challenge), with information on the most important trends and players, followed by detailed instructions on how the game will be played and how the teams will be divided up.

Students are not given any materials ahead of the event and are only vaguely aware of the details as to which industry the simulation will play in. The intention is to throw a considerable amount of information at the students, send them off to their breakout groups, ask them for ambitious deliverables, mix them up with people they have just met for the first time, and give them a very tight deadline. With some help from their coaches to keep them on schedule and making sure the minimum standards for the deliverables are met, the teams need to figure out quickly how they want to organize themselves, plan the available time, scan through the information, synthesize their findings and come up with an action plan to cover how they want to position themselves in the competitive context: not an easy task, but very typical for any type of consulting project. The coaches, all of whom have solid background knowledge of the industry and are experienced project managers, were available for individual questions, but were not allowed to contribute in the strategy formulation process.

Basically all the information the students may use is provided in the gamebooks and the use of PowerPoint presentations or internet research is not allowed (nor do they have the time for these). Past experience suggests that if PowerPoint were permitted the teams would focus too much on the look of their presentations at the expense of the quality of the content.

While the competitor teams are given the task of analyzing the information and coming up with a strategy for their respective moves, the market and control team, (which, for the sake of simplicity, are combined in this simulation) has the task of developing a market view. This view is based on customer segmentation and involves brainstorming and structuring a list of customer preferences in priority order per segment. This list will provide the basis for the subsequent evaluation of the competitive offerings for each move by the market on the basis of a system of scores. In order for these scores to work correctly and consequently generate gains or losses in market share, the control team also needs to set up a market model. This involves them adjusting the model to reflect the correct weights for each of the parameters, labeling them correctly and doing a few dry runs to ascertain that the computations are working. The model has been designed by wargaming experts and is based on the growth projections for the industry, which depending on the decisions of all teams can accelerate, decelerate or remain as projected. Based on the attractiveness of the individual offerings of each team, their relative share in this development can grow or shrink.

At the end of each move the competitor teams received qualitative and quantitative feedback from the market and control team. Using computations within the model, they receive detailed market share numbers, approximate margins and relative change information. The qualitative feedback consists of statements from the various customer segments; what they like or don't like about specific offerings. Sometimes, just to spice things up, the control team will introduce certain "shocks" or events designed to force the teams to address a specific issue. For example, unforeseen problems with hardware components which affect cost structures or require product recalls or breakthrough technological developments, if feasible.

Alternatively, shocks may be in the form of public concern over issues such as piracy, traffic accidents caused while listening to music on the go, and so on. Whatever the problem the teams need to address it in their subsequent presentation or risk the market not rewarding them as hoped. These interventions thus enable the control team to encourage the competing teams to focus on particular issues they may wish them to explore.

At the end of the CEO Challenge and once the quantitative results are in, the market and control team issue several awards to reflect the battle as fought with sticks of different length. If, for example, you are on the dominant Apple Team, losing only a little market share is quite an accomplishment, because you have successfully defended your position despite increased competition and may still make considerable profits. On the other hand, if you are a new entrant or a small player the question is much more one of survival and growing the business from nothing into something.

The basis for the awards may vary from highest market share, best profitability, best marketing campaign, most innovative product and so on. At the end of the event, students are asked to reflect once more on what they have recognized and what they have learned about the industry and about their teams.

This synthesis of views yields very interesting insights and in the past teams have actually predicted a number of the real developments to follow. For example, one team predicted the introduction of the iPhone, more than one year before this happened; another predicted the high-end top-quality positioning of Sony Ericsson leveraging their "Walkman" brand. They also predicted the move towards hybrid devices, i.e. the combination of phone, mp3 player and PDA, therefore concluding that the biggest threat for Apple and the iPod will come from the mobile phone manufacturers if they can get their act and their products together.

The CEO Challenge has turned into an amazing success story for Booz Allen Hamilton. Applications are skyrocketing: fewer than one in every ten students can be slotted in for one of the events. As predicted, almost all graduates have become valuable ambassadors communicating news about the event and the Booz Allen Hamilton name on campus. While participating in the event is still no guarantee that a student will make it into the firm, many of the participants are genuinely interested and if they do make it through the process and ultimately receive an offer, they typically take it.

So, in sum, the value of the event lies in the marketing promotion of the Booz Allen Hamilton brand and its people, but also in spotting top talent and being able to see how they work. A very valuable process when the alternative involves simply paper screens and a number of behavioral and case interviews. The costs for such an event are not trivial, but considering the quality of people a company can attract and the high likelihood of converting them into employees, the results repay the cost. The "halo" effect it has on the company's reputation at the top campuses is a free value add.

LESSONS LEARNED

It appeared that for the students, the major lesson learned is to focus on the customer and to formulate a consistent strategy which will stay valid over three moves and which would eventually generate market growth or contribute in general to the value of the played corporation. The following are quotes from students who participated in the CEO Challenge:

- "Spend lots of time on strategy and brainstorming. The more precisely you analyze and get your plan right upfront, the more efficient and hopefully successful you will be in the end."

- "Be efficient and collaborative and accept feedback given. The questions at hand are just too complex to try and tackle them as a one-man show."

- "Focus on customers, be aware that customers differ over time and that they need time to digest technological changes."

- "Understand position relative to competition. You can have a great value proposition to the customer. If your competitor has a better one, it is only worth half as much."

- "Understand how the market evolves, concerning technology, lifestyle, novelty, and commodity."

Testimonials of participating students illustrate how the business wargaming methodology represents a unique event, which is highly appreciated. One participant (Krasavin 2006, 2) summarized his experiences with the CEO Challenge in a report for his school and concluded:

> *The paragraph above illustrates what I love best about consulting — challenging problems that are solved by the team in an environment of high creativity and fun. As such and going back to the original purpose, the event was a tremendous success — we saw how Booz Allen Hamilton consultants work.*

What started within Booz Allen as a small initiative has established itself as a global top event on campuses.

Further Applications of Business Wargaming

CHAPTER

9

Thus far we have discussed a number of the current applications of business wargames and demonstrated how organizations can benefit from the methodology. In this chapter we explore two other fields where business wargaming can potentially make significant contributions—strategic early warning systems and corporate reputation management.

Strategic Early Warning Systems

There is evidence that most organizations lack the ability to spot relevant signals of change fast enough—in other words, to identify signals that announce opportunities or portend threats before the competition does so (Day and Schoemaker 2006). Fuld (2003) points out, based on a survey of 140 corporate strategists, that two thirds of those surveyed admitted that their organization had been surprised by as many as three high-impact competitive events in the past five years. Further, 97 percent of the surveyed stated that their organizations lacked the kind of early warning systems to avoid such surprises in the future. In a study done by Roland Berger Strategy Consultants (2003), the lack of a strategic early warning system was identified as one of the key causes of failure in strategic planning.

The concept of strategic early warning system (Schwarz 2005, 2006) can be seen as rooted in Ansoff's (1980) concept of strategic issue management. A strategic early warning system is a systematic procedure for early identification and fast response to important signals in the environment of an organization. The goal of a strategic early warning system is to detect early signals of change before they develop to a full crisis, or rather detect opportunities ahead of time compared to the competitors (Fuld 2003).

Two concepts are of particular importance for a strategic early warning system: the concept of weak signals (Ansoff 1975) and environmental scanning (Aguilar 1967). The underlying assumption of a strategic early warning system is that discontinuity does not emerge without warning. These warning signs can be described as weak signals. Weak signals, if undetected, may lead to strategic surprises, leading to an event, which has the potential to threaten an organization's strategy.

The objective of a strategic early warning system is to detect weak signals. Detecting these signals in an organization's environment is achieved by scanning its environment. Environmental scanning describes a process in which the environment of an organization is systematically scanned for relevant information. The purpose is to identify early signals of possible environmental change and to detect environmental change already underway (Lester and Waters 1989).

In the figure below the "ideal" process of a strategic early warning is taken from Liebl (2000), who describes a process of three phases. The first phase is characterized by the information gathering of weak signals, or rather trends and issues, which can be perceived as the relevant weak signals in a business environment. The scanning relies primarily on looking at various media sources, referring to the technique of content analysis (Nasbitt 1982). Monitoring trends and issues that have already drawn attention complements the scanning activity.

The second phase is the one of diagnosis, which is characterized, in turn, by three steps. The first step contains an in-depth analysis of the trend or issue, examining the core and the involved contexts of this phenomenon. The aim is to gain an idea of the possible potential of an issue or trend. The second step has several goals. Firstly, an attempt should be made to think creatively about how the particular trend or issue could evolve. Secondly, the character of the contexts needs to be examined in order to cluster several trends or issues, enabling you to understand the mutual influences trends and issues may have. Because of an organization's limited resources it is important during the final step of the diagnostic phase to identify and select those trends and issues that are particularly relevant. Finally, the third phase describes the formulation of appropriate strategies to react to the identified and as appropriately labeled trends and issues.

When executing a strategic early warning system the constant question is where to scan, or what focus to give the scanning activity. Typically, if a business wargame has been used, several fields of interest will have been identified which may either threaten the organization's strategy or offer a variety of opportunities now or in the future. These points of interest are an excellent input for a strategic early warning system. Using these points of interest,

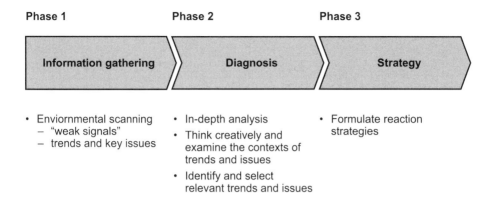

Phase 1   **Phase 2**   **Phase 3**

Information gathering   Diagnosis   Strategy

- Enviornmental scanning
  - "weak signals"
  - trends and key issues

- In-depth analysis
- Think creatively and examine the contexts of trends and issues
- Identify and select relevant trends and issues

- Formulate reaction strategies

Figure 9.1   The process of a strategic early warning system

derived from a business wargame, would not only allow such a system to gain a valuable input, it would also enable an organization to leverage the lessons learned and the experiences gained from a business wargame.

A business wargame can therefore be an excellent starting point for implementing a strategic early warning system, as it offers new insight and foresight to any system. Of course, in return the information gathered by a strategic early warning system may provide a wonderful source for designing a business wargame, leading in turn to greater foresight and hindsight, particularly if the aim of a business wargame is not simply to encounter and anticipate the competitor's behaviors, but, as Dunnigan (2000, 1) puts it, to "get a jump on the future."

Corporate Reputation Management: Stakeholder Wargame

Over the past decade managers, particularly in the US, came to realize that intangible assets could generate far more value for a corporation than the immediate benefits generated through patent protection or, for example, the acquisition of proprietary know-how about manufacturing processes, or special technologies.

Managers have recognized that the intangible asset of *corporate reputation* offers their companies a sustainable competitive advantage over their competitors as it generates greater sympathy with their current and future customers, employees, investors, and suppliers as well as the regulatory authorities, unions, public interest groups and so on.

Positive reputation may have several beneficial effects for the company, for example: an increased willingness amongst customers to buy the company's products, a desire amongst job seekers to work for the company, increased share values in the stock markets, and favorable relationships with public interest groups. These four benefits can be measured on the basis of repeat sales per customer, employee turnover, recruitment costs per candidate or price/earnings ratios in the stock markets. Corporate reputations are fragile and take a long time to build, but a few incidents of irresponsible behavior may destroy them.

By way of example, on March 24, 1989, the tanker Exxon Valdez was grounded on Bligh Reef in the upper part of the Prince William Sound. The tanker was carrying approximately 53 million gallons of crude oil, 11 million of which spilled into the Prince William Sound. Apart from the environmental catastrophe, the incident proved to be a huge setback for the Exxon corporation. Their slow and reactive crisis management lost them considerable goodwill amongst the general population and with environmental groups. The cost of the catastrophe was about one billion dollars in market capitalization during the period two weeks prior to and following the incident (Fombrun 1996).

In the Exxon case, contingency crisis planning both in terms of action and communication could have prevented at least some of the damage. This type of planning may have enabled Exxon to reassure the public about its concerns for the environment, and demonstrate decisiveness on the part of the company in preventing any further damage. The case illustrates that in order to protect a corporate reputation, a company needs a well-prepared crisis team and validated contingency plans. Such a system ensures the smooth running of the company, consistent behavior of the individuals working for the company, and consistent behavior of the company as a whole i.e. corporate behavior, whether or not the company faces a crisis or calm water.

Corporations and organizations are characterized by the fact that they are made up of people, acting together in order to pursue a common goal (Hodge, Anthony and Gales 1996). Inherent in this definition is the potential exposure of individual members of the organization to conflicts of interest between personal and organizational goals. During working hours, the members of an organization are expected to subordinate their personal goals to the goals of the organization.

The existence, or absence, of reputation can constitute a source of competitive advantage or disadvantage for a corporation in its market environment

(Fombrun 1996). If a corporation has a good reputation, it is likely to sell more to customers, receive more job applications, get more favorable coverage from financial analysts and journalists, and get more opportunities to enter business relationships with new customers, who have heard favorable things about it. A good corporate reputation, therefore, is one of the most valuable intangible assets to a company (Hall 1992, 1993). The accumulation of reputation capital (Fombrun 1996) is highly desirable, and thus a way to maximize firm value.

Both corporate and individual reputations are determined by actual or perceived actions. While in the case of an individual, these actions are driven by the individual's own behavior, in the case of organizations, they are made up of the collective behavior of the members. This collective behavior can be described as the sum of all individual behaviors of members of an organization.

Whilst an individual ultimately determines and is responsible for his or her own behavior, the collective behavior of an organization is at least in part a function of effective design and the influence of leadership. The bankruptcy cases of the Swiss national carrier Swissair and the energy giant Enron have shown more than once how fragile corporations are and the importance of effective governance systems to ensure smooth operations, as well as to guard against the fraudulent or negligent behavior of individuals or groups within the organization.

Wargaming may be used not only to prepare for crisis situations, but also run a sensitivity analysis around the major constituents of a corporation in order to better anticipate reputation risk factors. This could be by setting up the game revolving around the company and a handful of main competitors, and instead of just having a market team, actually playing different "response cells" such as a team representing the market, the workforce and their preference for each of the competitive teams as well as public interest groups and the investment community and where they would invest their money. The control team could probe for specific events that would have a potential impact on the reputations of the played companies such as product flaws, legal issues in the workplace, IT problems, boycotts etc. The objective would be to find out what the potential sensitivities are with the different stakeholders as well as training the participants in coming up with effective countermeasures to mitigate such reputational risks.

The difficulty may be that unless you understand the reputational risks for a company and their interdependencies in sufficient detail to quantify them, justifying the cost of a wargame may be hard work. On the other hand, any forward-looking manager should be concerned to take any conceivable measure to protect the reputation capital of his or her firm. If wargaming can help do this it will be a valuable tool for protecting corporate value.

An Alternative Approach to Designing a Business Wargame: Wargaming in the Automotive Industry

Pero Mićić[1]

This chapter describes a wargame in the automotive industry based around the concept of future management.

The Situation

One of the world's largest automotive suppliers wanted to analyze a number of dynamic competition scenarios for the business units of its most important division by means of a business wargame. A strategically significant acquisition made by a competitor had caught the executives by surprise and made them anxious to know more about potential competitors in the future. FutureManagementGroup AG was asked to prepare, facilitate and lead the wargame project.

Goals of the Wargame

The wargaming project was undertaken on the basis of four goals determined by the client following intensive discussions.

1.   To identify possible competitive situations and map competitor moves in the future.

2.   To reduce the number of blind spots in the top managers' perception.

1   Dr. Pero Mićić is the chairman of the FutureManagementGroup AG, Eltville, Germany.

3.   To strengthen the corporate strategy against the unexpected.

4.   To identify, develop and evaluate future opportunities.

IDENTIFY POSSIBLE COMPETITIVE SITUATIONS AND MAP COMPETITOR ACTIONS IN THE FUTURE

This primary goal was pursued and achieved by elaborating a series of competitive future scenarios which might evolve as a result of action and strategic moves by competitors. Since the probable and therefore most likely moves were already entirely known and had been thoroughly analyzed, the client was looking for those considerably less probable and more surprising future moves and situations with the strongest impacts. Despite the need to identify the unexpected, the moves and situations all needed to have a reasonable degree of plausibility.

REDUCE THE NUMBER OF BLIND SPOTS IN THE TOP MANAGERS' PERCEPTION

Blind spots are inevitable. Dangerous developments can evolve unnoticed by managers and catch the company by surprise. At the same time, blind spots hinder leaders' ability to discover new favorable developments and strategic opportunities in the business environment. It is impossible to get even close to a complete picture of all factors in the environment.

Blind spots are due to barriers to perception, awareness, imagination, and action which arise from a manager's lack of knowledge or intelligence and their inability to articulate ideas as well as their incorrect assumptions about reality and personal bias or aversions. All these factors can be situational and amplified by the individual's current state of mind. As a consequence, the consultants deliberately confronted the participants of the wargame with an unconventional design for their management meeting and with several challenges to commonly held beliefs.

STRENGTHEN THE CORPORATE STRATEGY AGAINST THE UNEXPECTED

Identifying blind spots, thereby reducing their number and developing eventual counter-strategies, implies making the corporate strategy more robust against the effects of possible surprise. One of the core purposes of future management is to enable management to be less likely to be surprised, which means looking for possible surprises and prepare yourself for them, at least mentally.

IDENTIFY, DEVELOP AND EVALUATE FUTURE OPPORTUNITIES

We define future opportunities as both the potential and the identified actions of an individual or an organization which are advantageous. The eventual plans developed to reinforce the strategy are a form of reactive opportunities. The alternative kind of future opportunities lies in the more active pursuit of possible advantageous strategies which are largely independent of the competitors' own decisions and actions. Such opportunities may originate as a result of the weaknesses or vulnerabilities of competitors, unmet customer demands, new technologies, or untapped markets.

TRIGGER CHANGE OF THE CORPORATE CULTURE

There was an additional goal which was particularly challenging with this client. The company's strategic behavior was and still is based on the values of good ethics and sustainability, as is the case with many traditional companies. Their behavior is correct, value driven and technology focused.

However, with more aggressive competitors from Western countries, let alone Asia, this kind of defensive culture was perceived as a dangerous weakness. Through the wargame managers were supposed to learn to embrace aggressive strategies without abandoning their values.

PLANNING AND PREPARATION

The wargame was organized as an intensive two-day workshop with 60 participants representing the entire top management of the company. There were simultaneous wargames involving three business units each with three competitors. Nine facilitators and nine documentators were needed for this setup, in addition to an overall facilitator for the entire group. The client chose to recruit half of the facilitators and recorders from their own staff and the other half from FutureManagementGroup. Figure 10.1 illustrates the process of the wargame.

A series of preparatory analyses were required in advance of the game:

1. Internal experts from the client's corporate intelligence departments helped identify the main trends in the automotive industry.

2. Another 39 future factors, for example trends, technologies and change drivers were chosen and prepared in the form of posters for the walls of the workshop rooms in order to expand the thinking horizon.

3.   We do not recommend you assume that the workshops will be spontaneously creative, so we prepared a list of 26 archetypal aggressive strategy moves, defining particular changes in value networks, pricing, acquisitions or niche strategies. These moves were designed to serve as templates for thinking on what the competitors or the company might possibly do in the future.

4.   A comprehensive profile was produced for each of the three competitors in each of the three business units. These nine profiles were summarized as nine one-page documents.

5.   The nine groups were formed: three market groups, each with three competitor groups. It was a particular challenge to mix participants within each group who had prior knowledge about the respective competitor(s) and market(s) with participants who had fresh minds.

6.   Facilitators and recorders were provided with a click-through presentation to help them structure and lead their workshops along with an electronic form to document the results. There was also a workshop booklet with a thorough description of the process and the rules to support the game and ensure good preparation.

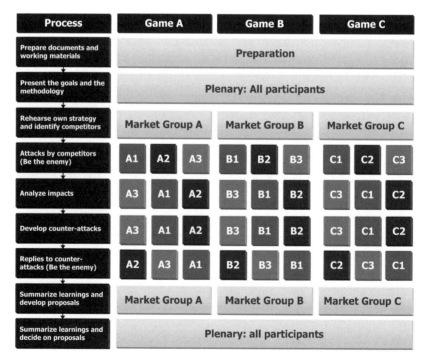

Figure 10.1   The process of the wargame

The preparatory work ended with a half-day workshop in which the project leaders, the facilitators and the recorders discussed and rehearsed the workshop process.

The Wargame

OPENING AND INTRODUCTION

The wargame took place in a secluded hotel which had enough rooms for the groups and the plenary sessions. The chief executive officer welcomed the participants, presented the core elements of the company's current strategy and provided the rationale for the wargaming project. The consultants set the scene with stories about wargames through history and in recent times as well as with a basic introduction to future management.

REHEARSAL OF THE PRESENT STRATEGY AND IDENTIFICATION OF COMPETITORS

The participants were acquainted with the structure of the groups and they were first sent as three market groups to their respective rooms. These groups rehearsed separately the business unit's current strategies. Questions from the participants, especially those from outside the unit, were answered in a brief session.

The three market groups were then split into three groups representing three types of competitors:

1. The company's main, actual, competitor in the market.

2. A potential new entrant from a related market.

3. A typical (and "virtual") competitor pursuing an aggressive low-cost strategy.

ROUND ONE: COMPETITOR ATTACKS ("BE THE ENEMY")

The group workshops were designed as simulated competitor strategy sessions. The working groups developed their moves and strategies based on the prepared material previously described. Each participant was assigned with a role within his or her group (e.g. operations manager of company A, marketing director of company B), which was documented with a corresponding name tag including the competitor's logo. "Be the enemy" was the guideline.

In order to increase the aggressiveness of their moves and strategies, competitors were assumed to have virtually unlimited funding by a notional investor. The main goal was to drive the (client) company out of the market with intelligent, effective, plausible and essentially legal moves and strategies. The moves and strategies were recorded as they were elaborated. The recorders used an electronic form in order to keep information flowing steadily throughout the process of interrelated workshops.

At the end of the first workshop (round one), a member of the group was appointed "ambassador." The ambassador was required to present the strategy to one of the other groups and to join this group during the second turn in order to explain the thinking and intentions of his or her original group through the presentation and written documentation.

ROUND TWO: DEFENSE AND COUNTER-ATTACKS

The goal of the second round was to develop strategies to counter the actions envisioned in round one. In this round the groups reverted back to their "real-life company." The ambassadors played the role of a high-level executive who had recently changed from working for the competitor to working for the company and brought inside information on the competitor's strategy, in order to present the strategies to the groups. The group then analyzed the impacts of this strategy.

This point represented the end of day one and the participants were given the opportunity to think about the impacts and possible elements for counter-strategies overnight. The following day, the working groups gathered to develop counter-strategies which might be either defensive or offensive. These elements were deliberately separated from the current strategy in order to provide more room for innovative approaches.

We identified seven typical ways to handle a possible surprise, once identified, as shown in Figure 10.2, and to develop eventual preventive or crisis strategies.

As before, the results were recorded and passed back to the competing group for the next turn.

ROUND THREE: RESPONSES TO COUNTER-ATTACKS

In round three the working groups reverted again to their role as the competitor from round one. The ambassadors returned to their original groups to play out

Approach	Explanation	Type
Neglect	Check and classify as not significant.	Preventive strategy
Prevent	Prevent the surprise from happening, by eliminating its prerequisites.	Preventive strategy
Provide	Develop an effective contingency plan in case the scenario comes true.	Preventive strategy
Prepare	Include defensive, securing or offensive elements in the present strategy.	Acute strategy
Convert	Convert the surprise into an opportunity as a jui-jitsu for your own benefit.	Acute strategy
Reduce	Reduce the potential loss or damage (e.g. by insurance).	Preventive strategy
Anticipate	Take the feared action yourself.	Preventive or acute strategy

Figure 10.2   General types of eventual strategies

the following scenario: the results of their strategy session were fortuitously transferred to the "own company." By chance the competitors received an intercepted email describing the company's counter-strategies. The ambassador filled the role of the person who received the email and presented the content, following which the impact was analyzed, the attack strategies adapted and further elements added.

IMPACT ANALYSIS

The impacts of the new strategies were again analyzed by the competitor groups. At this point the participants were allowed to abandon their roles and "become themselves again." They now agreed and recorded the most important lessons from their group. Following this the three working groups reformed in the market groups to present and discuss their lessons for the business unit and for the company as a whole. Finally, all three market groups rejoined the plenary session to summarize the findings for their business units and the whole company as well as the implications for the current strategy.

SUCCESS FACTORS FOR THE WARGAME

What was potentially the first critical success factor—the need to gain the top executives' time and attention—was irrelevant in this case since it was the CEO himself who had triggered the project. Consequently, the real first critical success factor was to achieve and maintain the kind of open mindset needed for a wargame of this kind. Many of the moves and strategies were extremely challenging since they went beyond the imagination of many of the participants. One example involved imagining a competitor who had developed an injection pump with a much lower pressure than is currently regarded as possible. It is only when participants focus their thinking on "why not" rather than on "that's impossible" that they achieve the prerequisite for lifting blinkers, opening their minds and expanding horizons of their thinking. The psychological problems associated with wargames are as follows:

1. *Probability thinking*: Participants tend to forget that they are supposed to look for the unexpected, which means setting aside the probable and look for improbabilities.

2. *Groupthink*: In common with many groups, executives suffer from a degree of groupthink which needs to be handled well by mixing the participants in the groups and by the facilitators asking awkward questions.

3. *Blind spots*: People cannot see what they do not know. Therefore the client searched to reduce the number and significance of blind spots as described in the goals above

4. *Experience-based thinking*: Executives, in particular, tend to rely heavily on their experience. However, experience can prevent them from imagining alternatives. This is the purpose behind mixing inexperienced *laymen* with the executives in each group.

5. *Craving the sensational*: People to attach meaning only to what is spectacular. However, it is often small, undervalued moves and developments which make the difference.

6. *Product focus*: Executives and technical executives tend to love their product(s). They need to be reminded that customers pay for functionality and benefits, not for products and not for solutions.

The second critical success factor involved managing the requisite complexity when 60 top executives were working in unfamiliar setups and in strange roles. Switching several times between different roles made the process even more challenging for everybody involved.

We managed to succeed thanks to long and thorough planning, preparation, and testing with all actors involved—with the exception of the executives themselves who were unavailable beyond just two interviews with the CEO. We developed a methodological model with suitable tools and techniques specifically for this project and we made sure that each group workshop was led by an experienced facilitator.

Lessons Learned

The executives identified several vulnerabilities in their strategy which they admitted had not been on their radar screen before. In addition, they discovered opportunities for improving their competitive position by anticipating the possible future actions of their competitors.

Results

The results of the wargame triggered several strategic initiatives to improve the company's strategy and to make it more robust against the impact of possible surprises. Several projects were started or changed to put the lessons learned and the new decisions into action. On the basis of the substantial results, similar wargaming projects were planned for other parts of the group.

PART III

Business Wargaming in Practice

Design and Execution

We have provided you with an overview of the history and the basic methodology of business wargaming and have given you insights into a number of past, present and future applications of it. We will now spend some time on how to design and execute business wargames. The specifics may vary significantly depending on the type of game and the underlying questions, which need to be answered, which means that this chapter can only offer a general guide to the process.

What follows is a pragmatic view of how to get from an initial idea to an executable business wargame and how the lessons learned are best captured. It is this capture of knowledge, which is a prerequisite to unlock the commercial value of any game and translate the learning into competitive advantage.

Any business wargaming follows a basic four-step process: design, preparation, execution, and debriefing/documentation. As displayed in Figure 11.1, each of these main work steps includes a variety of subactivities, which we will explain in more detail. By way of example we will relate the process to the application of business wargaming for strategy testing.

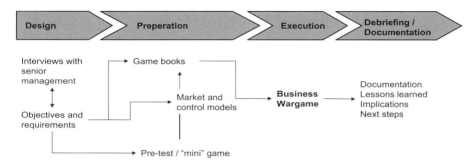

Figure 11.1   Process of designing and executing a business wargame

Source: Oriesek and Friedrich 2003, 68

Experience has shown that a typical strategy testing game can be put together and played over the course of approximately 8–12 weeks. The majority of the time required is used for preparing the game, collecting information, structuring the documents and setting up the models, boundaries, logistics and schedule. The 8–12 weeks' schedule assumes that a mixed team of consultants and clients work on setting up the game. Typically this will involve a senior wargaming expert and a project manager, as well as two or three consultants, who work together with a handful of client representatives. The overall time for preparing a game can be significantly reduced depending on how much competitive information is already available in the organization and how much work needs to be done to translate this data into game books and models.

During the execution phase of the game it is important that a larger consultant team, typically consisting of industry experts and at least one partner/principal per competitor team, be present. This larger team enables the client participants to focus on the task at hand without having to worry too much about process, timing, format of deliverables, communication with the other teams and the control team, and so on. Another benefit of working with a larger support team is that the partner and principals act as genuine coaches, who will not solve the problem for the teams, but will challenge their assumptions, throw in additional pieces of insight, and thus foster a productive work and team environment. The coaches also act as record keepers and are instrumental when preparing the debrief and summing up what actually happened in the various teams.

Design Phase

The most important aspect of the design phase is to determine the objectives of the game clearly and more specifically distil the key questions, to which the team will need to have found answers to by the end of the game. Perla (1990: 165), for instance, argues, when describing the objectives of a wargame:

> *In specifying the objectives, game sponsors, designer, and analysts must clearly identify how and in what ways the game can provide the type of experience and information needed to achieve them. The statement of objectives should be as specific as possible to allow game-design efforts to focus on those elements critical to the production of that experience and information, and to the assimilation of training lessons or the collection of research data. A wargame's objective should be the principal driver of its entire structure.*

Usually clients commissioning the design of a wargame have a broad idea of what they are seeking to discover through the game. As we have seen in Chapter Four, this may include questions such as: How best can we enter a market? Should we make use of a given technology (and if so, how)? Does an alliance or acquisition make sense? What will happen if some of the basis of current regulation changes? What will be the impact on our current business models or how might we change them? What should we do if …? How can we test a certain course of action? And so on.

Since wargames do not come cheap—the average sticker price for a fully fledged game, which is developed from scratch, is well in the half-a-million to million dollar range—the client sponsor often finds themselves in a dilemma. While they know that conducting a game will provide valuable insights and help the company avoid costly mistakes or optimize its strategy, conducting a game is an expensive process. Therefore the sponsor is taking a significant personal risk in proposing an exercise of this kind.

It is important therefore, as an early step that the consultants, often together with the sponsor, conduct a series of interviews with other members of the senior management team. These interviews will provide a wealth of expert views around the underlying question the game needs to answer which in turn generates a long list of detailed questions, all of which need to be answered. Involving the right internal stakeholders in this way ensures that the client sponsor and the game itself will have the necessary internal support and management attention to have a chance of success.

Ideally games should be commissioned by the CEO, a member of the board of directors, or a division head or business unit manager. However, on some occasions even functional managers, such as heads of business development, marketing directors or HR directors may opt to commission a game. The senior interviews are relatively informal, yet need to spend time on a number of topics, such as:

- What does the company want to learn from the business wargame?

- What are the key questions the wargame needs to answer?

- What are some of the most relevant and unaddressed issues in the organization?

- Who should participate in the process during the design and play stages? (From which business units, at what level and what should be their role in the exercise, i.e. experts vs. participants?)

- What is the focus of the game? Rather than trying to model every detail of the business, what products, stakeholders, competitors, customers segments and markets are most relevant in order to answer the set of questions?

- What should be the time horizon of the business wargame?

Answering these questions thoroughly and gaining a consensus view of the objectives is particularly critical for the success of any wargame. Unless top management is in favor of such a game, will dedicate the time and resources to it and is serious about participating in it even if this involves slipping into the role of competitors, the investment will be a waste of time from the outset.

Preparation

Once the design parameters have been set, you need to gather together the requisite information about the main competitors, the market(s), customers, current and pending regulation, technology trends, possible unexpected events and so on, which are then distilled into the gamebooks (basically the screenplays describing how to play the game) and into the market and control models, which are designed in order to provide some objective measures to key parameters for the game. The gamebooks contain information about the client company and the competitors in the game and a market overview, as well as the most important trends, regulation and technological developments in the industry.

The market models do not aim to capture everything that is happening in the real world, but are designed pragmatically around key aspects such as the main customer groups, essential financial data and so on which will be explored in the game. While models are important for their use as frameworks for what is happening in an industry, they are merely a support tool for the experts in the market and control teams, who will need to scrutinize their results in any event and, if necessary, adjust these in order to emphasize particular developments.

To give you a specific example: when simulating the portable audio device market in the United States for the Booz Allen Hamilton CEO Challenge, we prepared an elaborate model which used a wide variety of input parameters and ratings to enable experts from the market team to assign market shares and, at the second stage of the game, to calculate margins and net profitability for a number of products. The assumptions used in order to estimate the cost levels built into the model were based on industry research. This research estimates material cost and R&D cost at various levels, depending on whether we were dealing with an audio-only, mobile phone or hybrid product, based on certain assumptions around the quality of components.

On one occasion, a team took a very low-cost approach to the design of a mobile phone product, using cheap components and only basic functionalities requiring little R&D and so on. The model which assumed a specific cost level for this type of product generated a negative profit figure, on the basis of the price point at which the team intended to sell the product. This meant that the control team needed to adjust some of the component costs manually in order to do the product justice. Otherwise the team would not have been able to break even within the constraints of the model. This example illustrates how the model provides good direction, but needs a reality check by the experts on an individual product basis.

Once the basic model is in place, a so-called pre-test "mini" game should be conducted, in which the sensitivities of the model are tested and any bugs are detected and corrected. The "mini game" usually follows one or more likely scenarios, which reflect today's level of knowledge in the industry. The type of base scenario for the game depends on the objective of the wargame. If for instance, the aim is to prepare for crises or to assess the crisis management system of an organization, the scenario needs to be reasonably elaborate and will be introduced by the control team step by step.

If the focus is strategy testing, then the scenario may only consist of certain key developments, which are likely to take place over the course of the next couple of years. Take, for example, the opening up of the market for electricity. The scenario in this case may simply indicate that by the year X, the market for corporate clients will be open, followed two years later by the consumer market. A common framework is written on top of this basic scenario, based on what is known or assumed about market regulation. The framework is introduced as a set of guidelines for all players to follow. Beyond that the teams are free to do whatever they want within the boundaries of reality (defined by regulation and their own financial strength and capabilities).

All games have a common starting point of today, unless you deliberately choose to set at a different timeframe. What is known in reality today is also what is known in the game. However, from the second move on anything goes as long as it is within the boundaries set by the control team. The interesting thing is that at the outset of the game, even the game developers do not know where the game will be going after move two. It is also interesting that if one and the same game framework is given to two different participant groups, the game may develop quite differently, yet the lessons learned will be similar—as was demonstrated in the game series dealing with global power shifts which was conducted by the US government in the 1980s. The outcome of the initial game seemed so implausible that the game was repeated several times only to repeat the same outcome each time.

So the preparation phase provides the data set and rules for the game, which are important to structure the game and make sure it can be kept on track and focused on the questions relevant to the client. The objective of the rules are to keep the game close to reality and also keep the game playable, avoiding a wargame that becomes so complex that no one understands what they are doing. The trick is to give the teams plenty of leeway within the rules so they can experiment with everything that would be available to them in the real world. In order to keep the balance between playability and complexity, the control team needs to be experienced in running games, but also possess a profound understanding of the industry and market so that it can take corrective actions should they become necessary.

In order to get the most out of the game, the participants, regardless of their team, need to receive a proper briefing. This briefing, which can make up the last step of the preparation or the first step during the game's execution, will set the common ground for all parties involved. During the briefing the teams receive a crash course in strategy and wargaming; typically including a high-level summary of industry trends and facts, which may include a detailed competitor briefing as well a detailed explanation on how to play the game. During the "how to play the game" part of the session, participants are divided into the various teams, assigned coaches and familiarized with the expected deliverables, how to communicate with other teams and the market and given a very detailed schedule.

Execution

The execution of the game is the fun bit. Typically three moves are played out and the teams are busy trying to meet their schedule. In Chapter Two we provided a detailed description of what happens during a wargame, but it is worth emphasizing some points at this stage. First of all, although it is called *game*, this is serious business and it is of utmost importance to the success of the exercise that every individual involved gives the game their best shot and tries to live the role they have been assigned. Only if the competitors try their very best to beat their real-life company will they create the necessary pressure that will drive their peers in the company team to perform at their best. Switching roles and viewing the company from the perspective of competitors is itself enlightening and helps many long-term managers take a fresh look at what their company is good at and where it can improve. In this sense business wargaming is also a means to overcome organizational blindness.

The second important aspect for successful execution is to stick with the schedule and agreed deliverables. There is nothing more annoying than a situation in which four out of five teams are on time and deliver their solution to the agreed level of quality while one team then lags behind. If this happens the entire wargame is in danger of running out of sync, which will jeopardize the objectives. For this reason, wargames are ideally conducted by a dedicated team of experts and supported by experienced coaches, who can keep an eye both on the clock and on the quality of the deliverables. Typically you need to present an initial summary of the lessons learned after each move and certainly at the end of the actual game (which usually lasts between two and three days). This summary is assembled from the observations of the coaches and the control team as well as from the input provided by the participants.

Debriefing and Documentation

Arguably the most important part of any wargaming exercise, the detailed debriefing, happens around a week following the actual game. Based on the coaches' observations, input from participants and hard data provided through the models and evaluation of all the email traffic throughout the moves, the consultants compile what could be called the core results of the game. This includes a list with the most important observations made during the game, followed by what could be learned from these observations and what the consequences are for the client company. Based on this deductive approach, you can formulate a set of specific recommendations, which it is to be hoped will find their way back into the original strategic plan to enable you to improve it or to avoid any undesirable outcomes or take certain action, such as acquiring a competitor, launching a new technology, or entering new markets. The depth and focus of the debriefing is again dependent on the objectives of the game, Steinwachs (1992), for instance, provides several examples of how to go about debriefing a simulation. In a strategy testing game, the debriefing follows the just described path, while in a crisis prevention game typically an action plan or contingency plans are developed. In educational games, the debriefing may have a stronger focus on the group dynamics and what the key points were in the decision process, where the group took quantum leaps or why mistakes were made.

Summary

At this point, we would like to summarize what we believe are the critical success factors for designing and executing a successful business wargame:

- *Tailor-made for each client*: Business wargames should be tailor-made for each client and should reflect the overarching objective, issues, and questions of that particular client.

- *Thorough preparation*: Preparation is critical and starts with in-depth interviews with principal players prior to the wargame. Once buy-in is obtained, thorough work needs to go into the preparation of the gamebook and models.

- *Solid quantitative data*: Ideally a wargame should have solid quantitative data. If this is not possible, it should always provide a framework to allow you to reverse engineer why certain things turned out the way they did.

- *Pragmatic models*: Models should be comprehensive, but focus on the key questions and reduce complexity rather than trying to model everything that is happening.

- *Intensive and well structured*: Good business wargames are intensive, but also fun for the participants. They are tightly scheduled with clear deliverables and a professional team to run and coach the game. In this way the participating managers can fully submerge themselves in the experience and actually live through a likely future.

- *Close to reality*: The better participants identify with their roles, the better the mutual learning experience. It is the role of the facilitators to set the stage and make sure participants are motivated and well prepared to take on their roles. The facilitators also need to stay on top of all the actions and keep the participants within the boundaries of reality.

- *Follow through*: Each wargame must have a proper debrief. Without a debrief, lessons learned and an action plan it is nothing more than a game and of little use to the client.

Done well, participants and companies will get a great deal out of a wargame. The most valuable aspect in our view is the unique ability to go through a shared experience of seeing what is likely to happen. Managers will see together what works well and what does not and learning takes place in the group. It is not unusual that the energy experienced during a game will continue to have a positive effect in facilitating cooperation within and across departments. We believe the main drivers for this process are the intense experience shared, the mutual learning and the common ground established during the game and particularly during the debrief.

Bibliography

Aguilar, F.J. (1967), *Scanning the Business Environment* (New York: The Macmillan Company).

Ahlquist, G. and Burns, H. (2002), 'Bioterrorism Wargame', www.boozallen. com/media/file/103349.pdf.

Andlinger, G.R. (1958), 'Looking Around: What Can Business Games Do?', *Harvard Business Review* 36:4, 147–52.

Ansoff, H.I. (1975), 'Managing Strategic Suprise by Response to Weak Signals', *California Management Review* XVIII:2, 21–33.

Ansoff, H.I. (1980), 'Strategic Issue Management', *Strategic Management Journal* 1:2, 131–48.

Bazerman, M.H. and Watkins, M.D. (2004), *Predictable Surprises* (Boston MA: Harvard Business School Press).

Bell, W. (2003), *Foundations of Futures Studies, Vol. 1* (New Brunswick NJ: Transaction Publishers).

Booz Allen Hamilton (2004), 'The AIDS Epidemic: A Strategic Simulation', www.boozallen.com/media/file/137999.pdf.

Bracken, P. (2001), 'Business War Gaming', *Scenario & Strategy Planning* 3:2, 15–18.

Bracken, P. and Shubik, M. (2001), 'War Gaming in the Information Age', *Naval War College Review* LIV:2, 47–60.

Brewer, G.D. and Shubik, M. (1979), *The War Game* (Cambridge MA: Harvard Univeristy Press).

Broomley, D.B. (1993), *Reputation, Image and Impression Management* (Chichester: John Wiley & Sons).

Caffrey Jr, M. (2000), 'Toward a History-Based Doctrine for Wargaming', *Aerospace Power Journal* XIV:3, 33–56.

Courtney, H. (2001), *20/20 Foresight: Crafting Strategy in an Uncertain World* (Boston MA: Harvard Business School Publishing).

Day, G.S. and Schoemaker, P.J.H. (2006), *Peripheral Vision: Detecting the Weak Signals That Will Make or Break Your Company* (Boston MA: Harvard Business School Press).

Duck, J.D. (2001), *The Change Monster* (New York: Crown Business).

Dunnigan, J.F. (2000), *Wargames Handbook* (New York: Writers Club Press).

Eden, C. and Ackermann, F. (1998), *Making Strategy* (London: Sage Publications).

Faria, A.J. and Dickinson, R. (1994), 'Simulation Gaming for Sales Management Training', *Journal of Management Development* 13:1, 47–59.

Feldmann, J. and Krüger, P. (2007), *Die Systematik der strategischen Führung* (Frauenfeld: Huber).

Fombrun, C. (1996), *Reputation - Creating Value from the Corporate Image* (Boston MA: Harvard Business School Press).

Fuld, L. (2003), 'Be Prepared', *Harvard Business Review* 81:11, 20–21.

Fuld, L. (2006), *The Secret Language of Competitive Intelligence* (New York: Crown Business).

Fuller, T. and Loogma, K. (2007), 'Constructing Futures; a Social Constructionist Perspective on Foresight Methodology', paper presented at the COAST A22 Conference 'From Oracles to Dialogue; Exploring New Ways to Explore the Future', Athens, Greece.

Gilad, B. (2004), *Early Warning: Using Competitive Intelligence to Anticipate Market Shifts, Control Risk, and Create Powerful Strategies* (New York: AMACOM).

Ginter, P.M. and Rucks, A.C. (1984), 'Can Business Learn from Wargames?', *Long Range Planning* 17:3, 123–8.

Grant, R.M. (2003), 'Strategic Planning in a Turbulent Environment: Evidence from the Oil Majors', *Strategic Management Journal* 24:6, 491–517.

Haffa, R.P. and Patton, J.H. (1999), 'The Need for Joint Wargaming: Combining Theory and Practice', *US Army War College* 29:3, 106–18.

Hall, R. (1992), 'The Strategic Analysis of Intangible Resources', *Strategic Management Journal* 13:2, 135–44.

Hall, R. (1993), 'A Framework Linking Intangible Resources and Capabilities to Sustainable Advantage', *Strategic Management Journal* 14:8, 607–18.

Hamel, G. and Prahalad, C.K. (1994), *Competing for the Future* (Boston MA: Harvard Business School Press).

Hartung, A. (2004), 'Quotes: Pithy Sayings for the New World of Work', www.thephoenixprinciple.com/quotes/.

Hodge, B.J., Anthony, W.P. and Gales, L.M. (1996), *Organizing Theory: A Strategic Approach* (Upper Saddle River NJ: Prentice Hall).

Jarrett, M. (2003), 'The Seven Myths of Change Management', *Business Strategy Review*, 14:4, 22–9.

Kalman, J.C. and Rhenman, E. (1975), 'The Role of Management Games in Education and Research', in Greenblat, C.S. and Duke, R.D. (eds), *Gaming-Simulation: Rationale, Design, and Application* (New York: Sage Publication), 233–69.

Krasavin, A. (2006), 'The Insider's View of Consulting: Booz Allen Hamilton's CEO Challenge', students.som.yale.edu/sigs/Euro/AK/BAH_CEO_Challenge _Writeup_Krasavin.pdf.

Kurtz, J. (2002), 'Introduction to Business Wargaming', *Competitive Intelligence Magazine* 5:6, 23–8.

Kurtz, J. (2003), 'Business Wargaming: Simulations Guide Crucial Strategy Decisions', *Strategy & Leadership* 31:6, 12–21.

Lester, R. and Waters, J. (1989), *Environmental Scanning and Business Strategy* (Cambridge: University Press).

Liebl, F. (2000), *Der Schock des Neuen: Entstehung und Management von Issues und Trends* (München: Gerling Akademie Verlag).

Lüchinger, R. (2001), *Der Fall der Swissair* (Zürich: Bilanz Verlag).

Makridakis, S. (2004), 'Foreword: Foresight Matters', in Tsoukas, H. and Shepherd, J. (eds), *Managing the Future* (Oxford: Blackwell Publishing), XIII–XIV.

McCown, M.M. (2005), 'Strategic Gaming for the National Security Community', *Joint Force Quarterly* 39, 34–9.

McKenna, T. (2003), 'This Means War', *The Journal of Electronic Defence*, December 42–6.

Merriam-Webster's (1994), *Merriam-Webster's College Dictionary* (Springfield IL, Merriam-Webster).

Mitroff, I.I. (2000), *Managing Crises Before they Happen* (New York: Amacom).

Mitroff, I.I., Pearson, C.M. and Harrington, L.K. (1996), *The Essential Guide to Managing Corporate Crises* (New York: Oxford University Press).

Nasbitt, J. (1982), *Megatrends*. (New York: Warner Books).

Oriesek, D.F. and Friedrich, R. (2003), 'Blick in die Zukunft', *Harvard Business Manager*, May 65–71.

Perla, P.P. (1990), *The Art of Wargaming* (Annapolis MD: Naval Institute Press).

Rigby, D. (2005), *Management Tools 2005: An Executive's Guide* (Boston MA: Bain & Company).

Rodriguez, R. (2006), 'Creating an Employment Brand for Your Organi- zation', *Talent Management*, www.talentmgt.com/recruitment_retention/2006/ November/196/index.php.

Roland Berger Strategy Consultants (2003), *Excellence in Strategic Planning: Roland Berger Studie über die strategische Planung* (München: Roland Berger Strategy Consultants).

Rubel, R.C. (2006), 'The Epistemology of War Gaming', *Naval War College Review* 59:2, 108–28.

Schoemaker, P.J.H. (1992), 'How to Link Strategic Visions to Core Capabilities', *Sloan Management Review* 34:1, 67–81.

Schwarz, J.O. (2005), 'Pitfalls in Implementing a Strategic Early Warning System', *Foresight* 7:4, 22–30.

Schwarz, J.O. (2006), *The Future of Futures Studies: A Delphi Study with a German Perspective* (Aachen: Shaker).

Senge, P.M. (1990), *The Fifth Discipline* (London: Century Business).

Starr, S.H. (2001), 'Good Games: Challenges for the War-Gaming Community', *Naval War College Review* LIV:2, 89–97.

Steinwachs, B. (1992), 'How to Facilitate a Debriefing', *Simulation & Gaming* 23:2, 186–95.

The Thought Leadership Summit (2006), 'Reinventing Distribution: The Future of Asset Management', www.tls-reedmidem.com/files/TLS2/ThoughtsandFindingsFulDocument.pdf.

Toffler, A. (2000), 'Interview with Alvin Toffler', *Business 2.0*, September.

Treat, J.E., Thibault, G.E. and Asin, A. (1996), 'Dynamic Competitive Simulation: Wargaming as a Strategic Tool', *Strategy, Management, Competition*, Second Quarter, 46–54.

Tsoukas, H. (2004), 'Coping with the Future: Developing Organizational Foresightfulness', *Futures* 36:2, 137–44.

van der Heijden, K. (1998), 'Articulating the Business Idea: The Key to Relevant Scenarios', in Fahey, R. and Randall, R.M. (eds), *Learning from the Future: Competitive Foresight Scenarios* (San Francisco CA: John Wiley & Sons), 335–51.

van der Heijden, K., Bradfield, R., Burt, G., Crains, G. and Wright, G. (2002), *The Sixth Sense* (Chichester: John Wiley & Sons).

Vanderveer, R. and Heasley II, J. (2005), 'War Gaming: Exercises in Defending Brand Territory', *MM&M*, May, 68–72.

Watman, K. (2003), 'War Gaming and its Role in Examining the Future', *Brown Journal of World Affairs* 10:1, 51–61.

Index

business wargames
    business school games, differences 21–2
    crises management 57–9
business wargaming
    as accelerated learning xiii
    applications 39–55, 99–104
    automotive industry 105–13
    benefits xiii, 1, 33–5, 42
    change management 81–3
    company team 23–4
    competitor teams 24
    control team 25
    corporate reputation management 102–3
    cost 2, 34
    definition 1, 21–2
    design/execution 117–25
    education/recruitment 85–97
    elements 23–5
    evolution 18–20
    examples 22–3, 34–5
    foresight development 74
    interactions 25–6
    learning focus 19
    market team 24–5
    methodology 21–35
    military wargames, similarities 18
    moves 26–8
    prerequisites 1
    strategic focus 19–20
    teams 23–5
    types 39
    and uncertainty 1
    in universities 20, 88–91

CEO Challenge game
    awards 95
    background 92
    Booz Allen Hamilton 91–7, 120
    game setup 93–6
    lessons learned 96–7
    objective 92–3
    recruitment 91–3, 96
    teams 94–5
change, phases 81
change management 81–3
    plastics company 82–3
Chaturanga game 8
chess 8–9
China 79
company team, role 23–4

competitor teams, role 24
computer simulations 21–2
computer wargames 15, 17, 18
Confederation of Indian Industry, HIV/
    AIDS game 61, 62, 63
control teams, role 25
corporate culture 107
corporate reputation management 101–4
    business wargaming 102–3
    sensitivity analysis 103
corporate strategy 106
Council for Excellence in Government,
    bioterrorism game 68
crisis management 57–9
crisis response preparation 57–72
    case studies 59–72
crisis strategies 111
customer focus 96

design/execution, business wargame 117–25
    briefing 122
    cost 119
    debriefing/documentation 117, 123–4
    design 117, 118–20
    execution 117, 118, 122–3
    key questions/objectives 118–20
    pre-testing 121
    preparation 117, 118, 120–2
    process 117
    rules 122
    strategy testing 121
    success factors 124–5
    timeframe 121–2

education see management education
Enron bankruptcy 103
European Economic Area 43
European Union 43
Exxon Valdez incident 102

financial information game
    background 59
    game setup 60
    key questions/objectives 59
    lessons learned 61
    terrorism scenario 59–60
Firefight game 17
foresight
    and corporate success 74
    definition 73–4

About the Authors

Daniel F. Oriesek

Daniel F. Oriesek received his BSc in business administration from City University in Zürich, his MBA from the Stern School of Business at New York University and his PhD from Southern California University for Professional Studies. He is a Principal with A.T. Kearney in Switzerland and consults national and international clients on a variety of topics, including business wargaming. Prior to joining A.T. Kearney, Daniel worked for Russell Reynolds Associates and before that held leadership roles and worked for consulting firm Booz Allen Hamilton, where he was also a member of the firm's global commercial wargaming team. Before joining Booz Allen, Daniel worked for UBS in Zürich and New York, where he had different roles in private banking and asset management. Daniel holds the rank of Major of the General Staff in the Swiss Armed Forces, is married and has two sons.

Jan Oliver Schwarz

Jan Oliver Schwarz holds an MA in general management from the University of Witten/Herdecke, Germany, and a MPhil in futures studies from the Graduate School of Business, University of Stellenbosch, South Africa. Besides working on his PhD in strategic foresight, Jan has published numerous articles on strategic foresight and applies business wargaming for teaching master-level students across Europe.

If you would like to comment on the book, get in touch with us or keep informed on our activities concerning business wargaming, please refer to www.business-wargaming.com.